STAR WARS

CLONE WARS

ADVENTURES

VOLUME 8

designers
Darin Fabrick and Josh Elliott

assistant editor
Dave Marshall

editor
Jeremy Barlow

publisher
Mike Richardson

Special thanks to Elaine Mederer, Jann Moorhead, David Anderman,
Leland Chee, Sue Rostoni, and Amy Gary at Lucas Licensing

The events in these stories take place
sometime during the Clone Wars.

Published by
Dark Horse Books
A division of Dark Horse Comics, Inc.
10956 SE Main Street
Milwaukie, OR 97222

darkhorse.com
starwars.com

To find a comics shop in your area, call the
Comic Shop Locator Service toll-free at 1-888-266-4226

First edition: May 2007
ISBN: 978-1-59307-680-1

5 7 9 10 8 6 4
Printed at Midas Printing International, Ltd., Huizhou, China

STAR WARS: CLONE WARS ADVENTURES VOLUME 8

STAR WARS®

CLONE WARS
ADVENTURES
VOLUME 8

VERSUS
script and art **The Fillbach Brothers**
colors **Tony Avina**

OLD SCORES
script **Chris Avellone**
art **The Fillbach Brothers**
colors **Pamela Rambo**

ONE OF A KIND
script **Jason Hall**
art **Ethen Beavers**
colors **Ronda Pattison**

PATHWAYS
script **Jeremy Barlow**
art **The Fillbach Brothers**
colors **Dan Jackson**

lettering
Michael Heisler

cover
The Fillbach Brothers and Dan Jackson

Dark Horse Books®

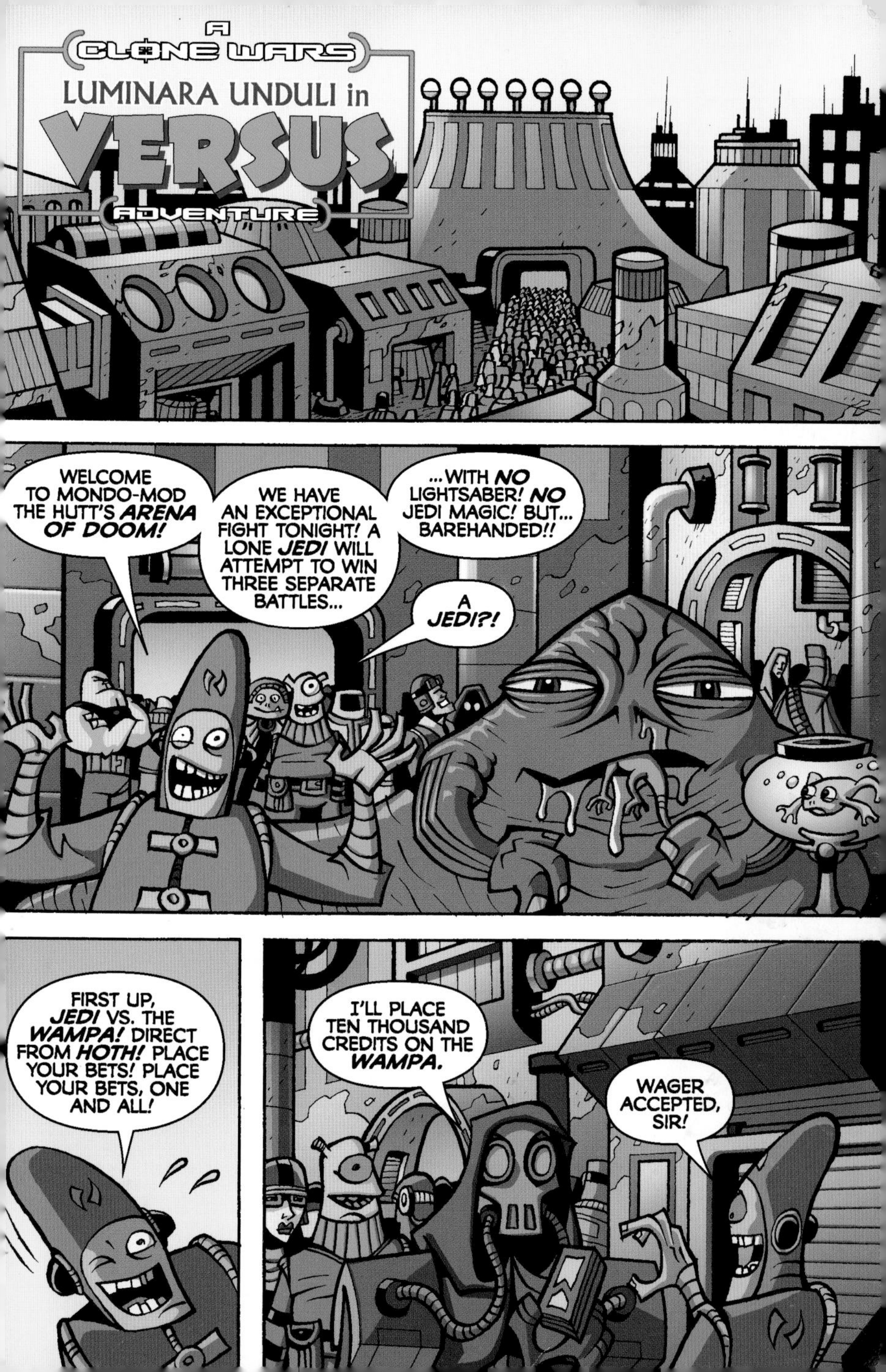
A CLONE WARS
LUMINARA UNDULI in
VERSUS
ADVENTURE
WELCOME TO MONDO-MOD THE HUTT'S ARENA OF DOOM!
WE HAVE AN EXCEPTIONAL FIGHT TONIGHT! A LONE JEDI WILL ATTEMPT TO WIN THREE SEPARATE BATTLES...
...WITH NO LIGHTSABER! NO JEDI MAGIC! BUT... BAREHANDED!!
A JEDI?!
FIRST UP, JEDI VS. THE WAMPA! DIRECT FROM HOTH! PLACE YOUR BETS! PLACE YOUR BETS, ONE AND ALL!
I'LL PLACE TEN THOUSAND CREDITS ON THE WAMPA.
WAGER ACCEPTED, SIR!

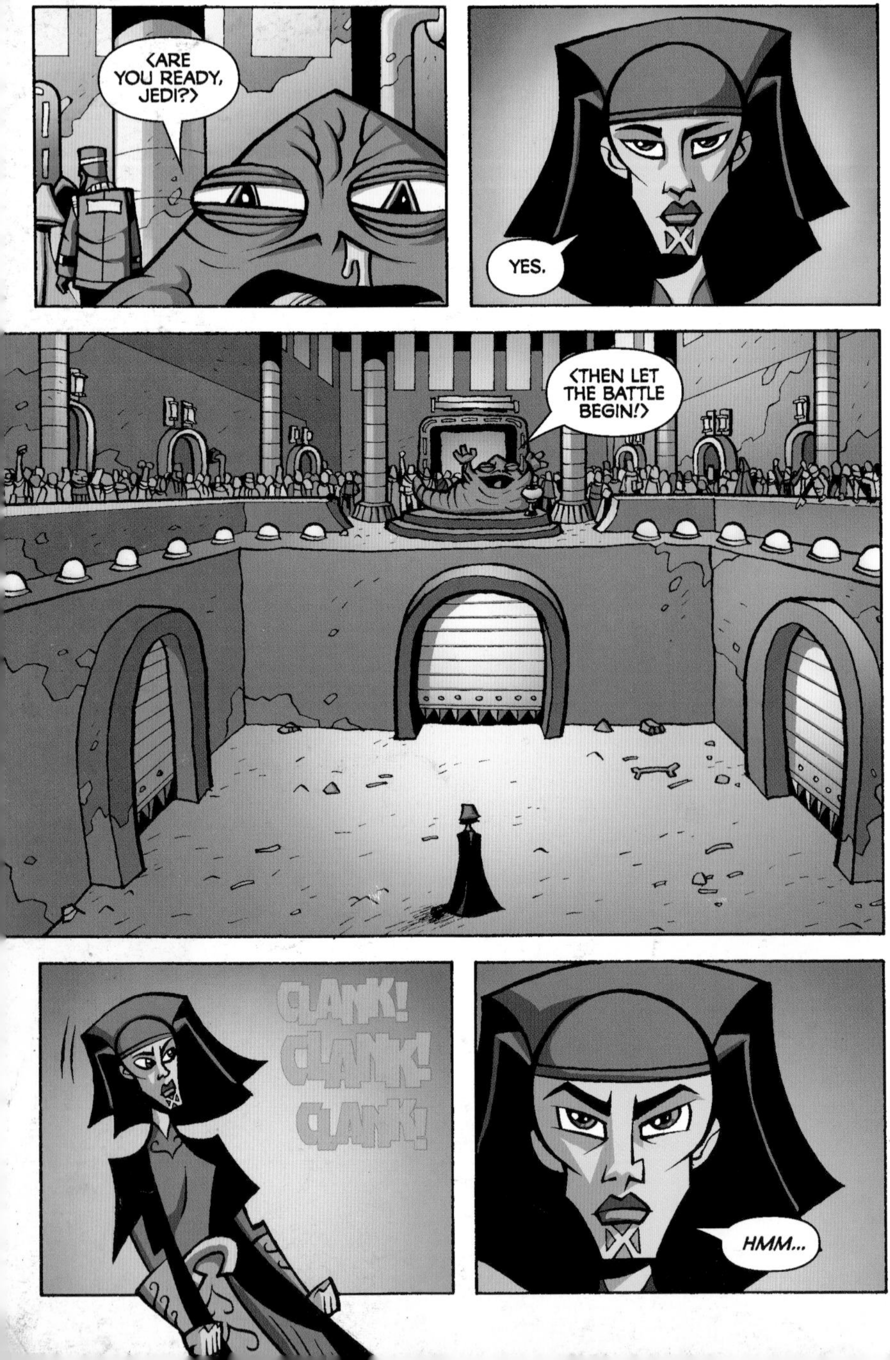
<ARE YOU READY, JEDI?>
YES.
<THEN LET THE BATTLE BEGIN!>
CLANK!
CLANK!
CLANK!
HMM...

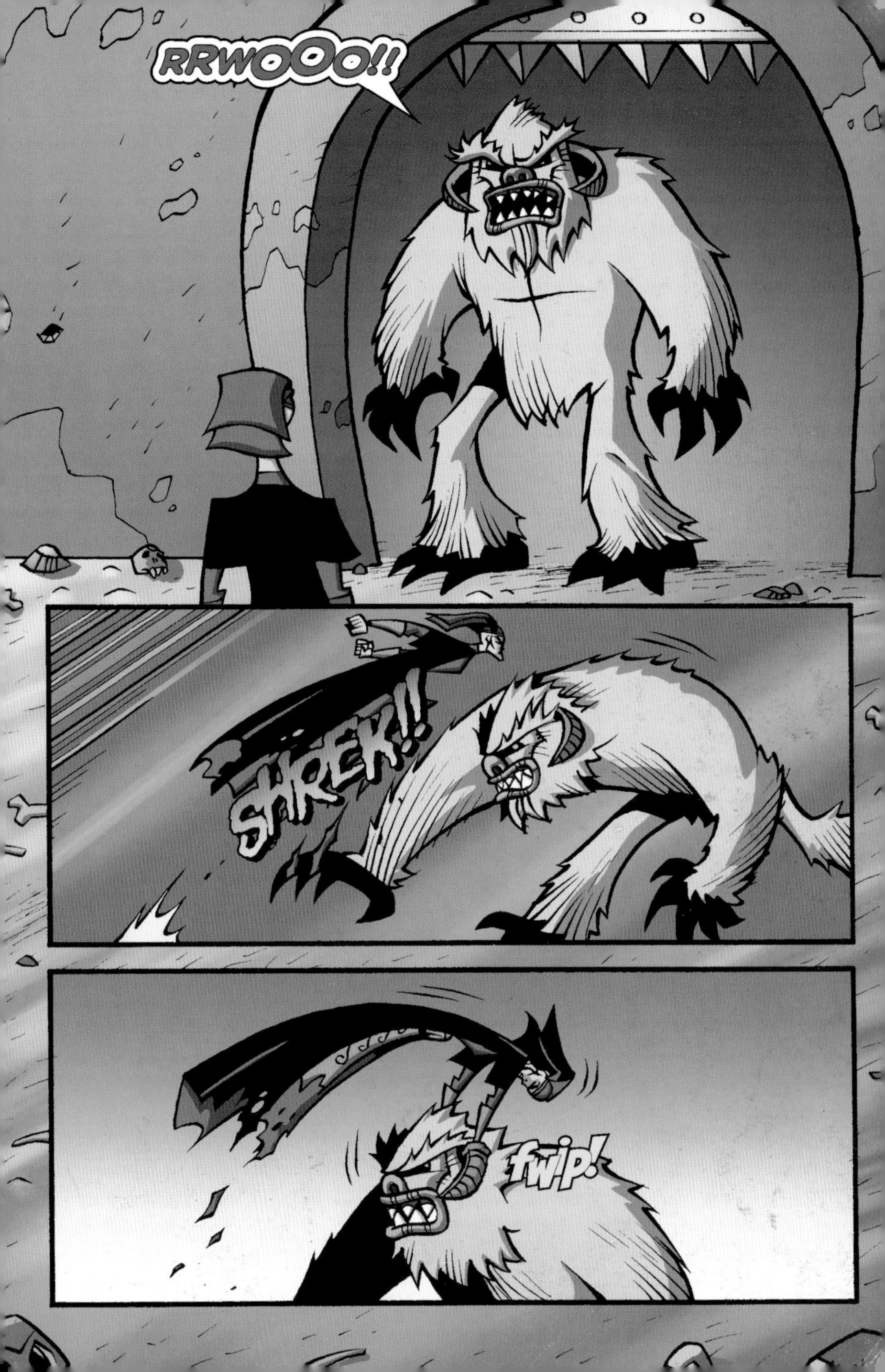
RRWOOOO!!
SHREK!!
fwip!

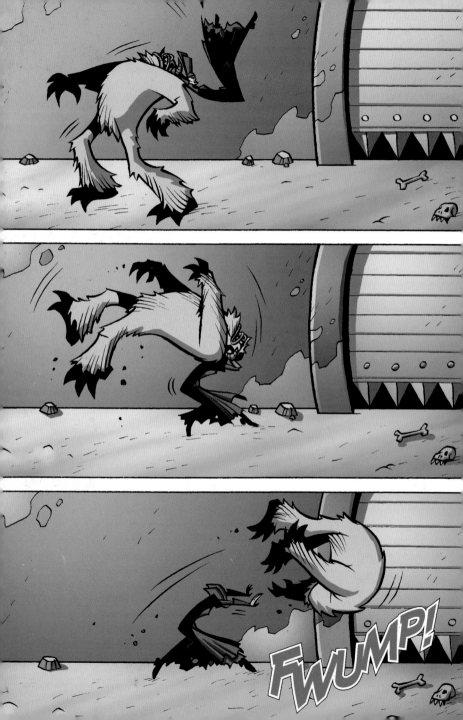

FWUMP!

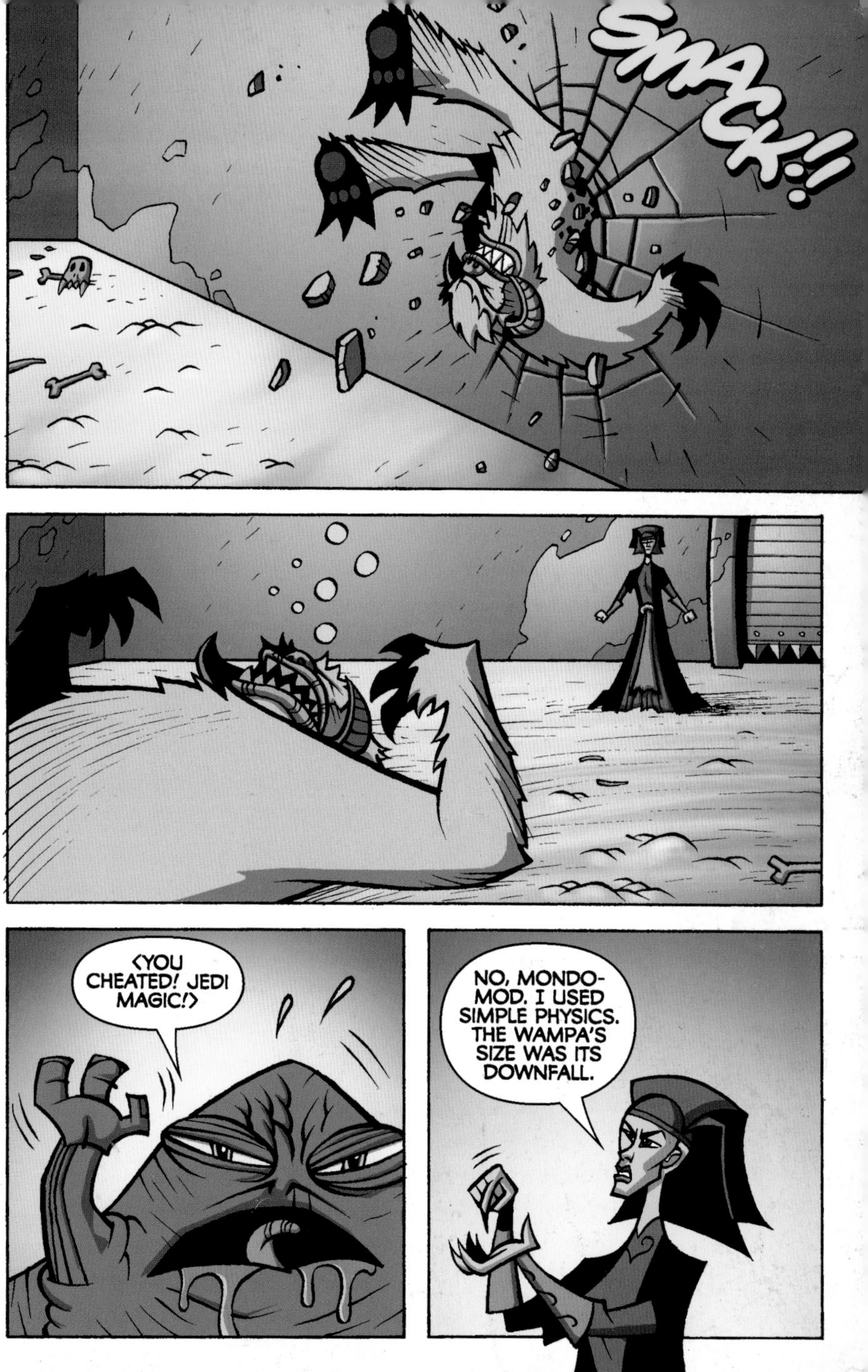
SMACK!!
<YOU CHEATED! JEDI MAGIC!>
NO, MONDO-MOD. I USED SIMPLE PHYSICS. THE WAMPA'S SIZE WAS ITS DOWNFALL.

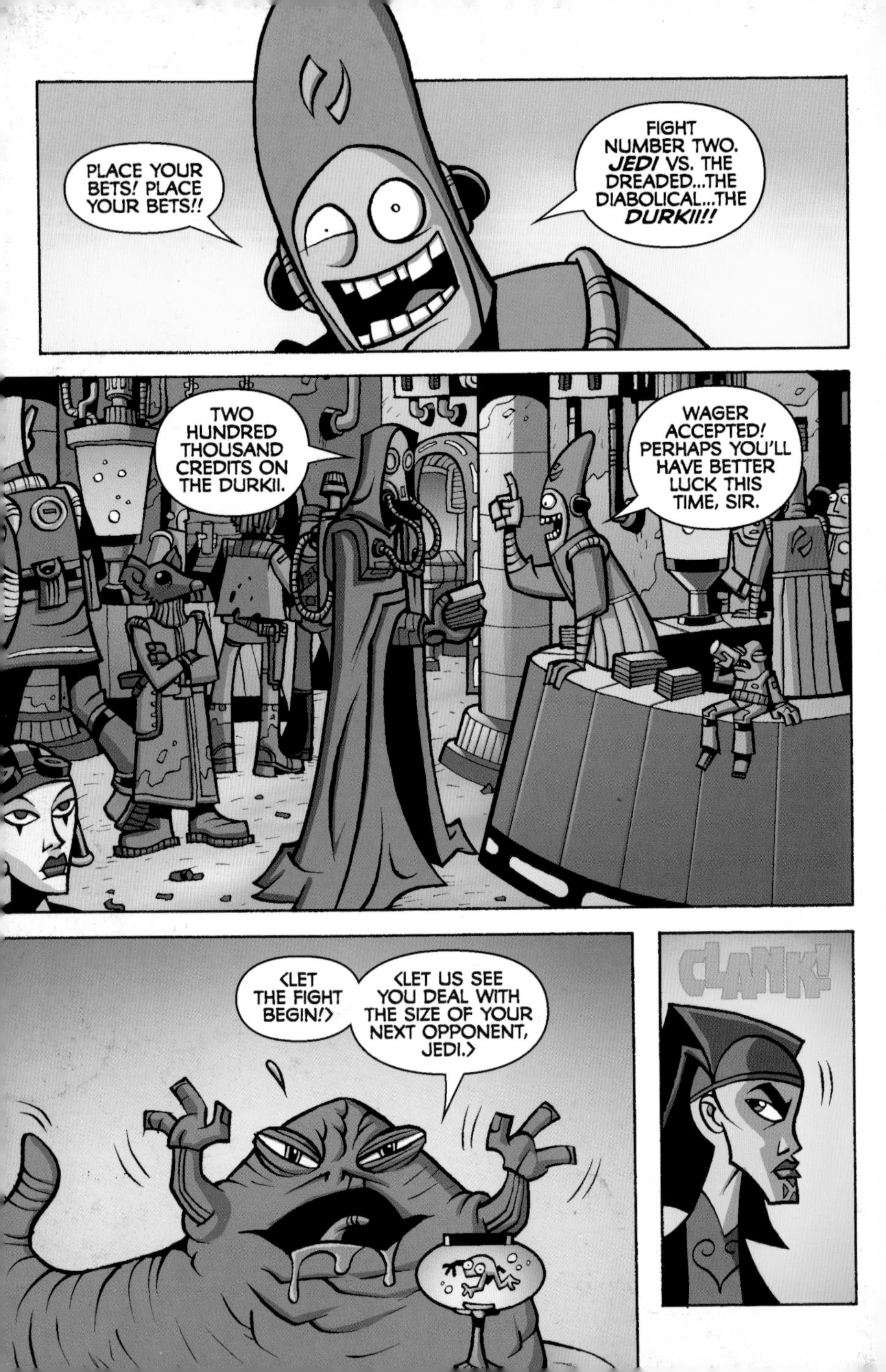
PLACE YOUR BETS! PLACE YOUR BETS!!
FIGHT NUMBER TWO. JEDI VS. THE DREADED...THE DIABOLICAL...THE DURKII!!
TWO HUNDRED THOUSAND CREDITS ON THE DURKII.
WAGER ACCEPTED! PERHAPS YOU'LL HAVE BETTER LUCK THIS TIME, SIR.
<LET THE FIGHT BEGIN!>
<LET US SEE YOU DEAL WITH THE SIZE OF YOUR NEXT OPPONENT, JEDI.>
CLANK!

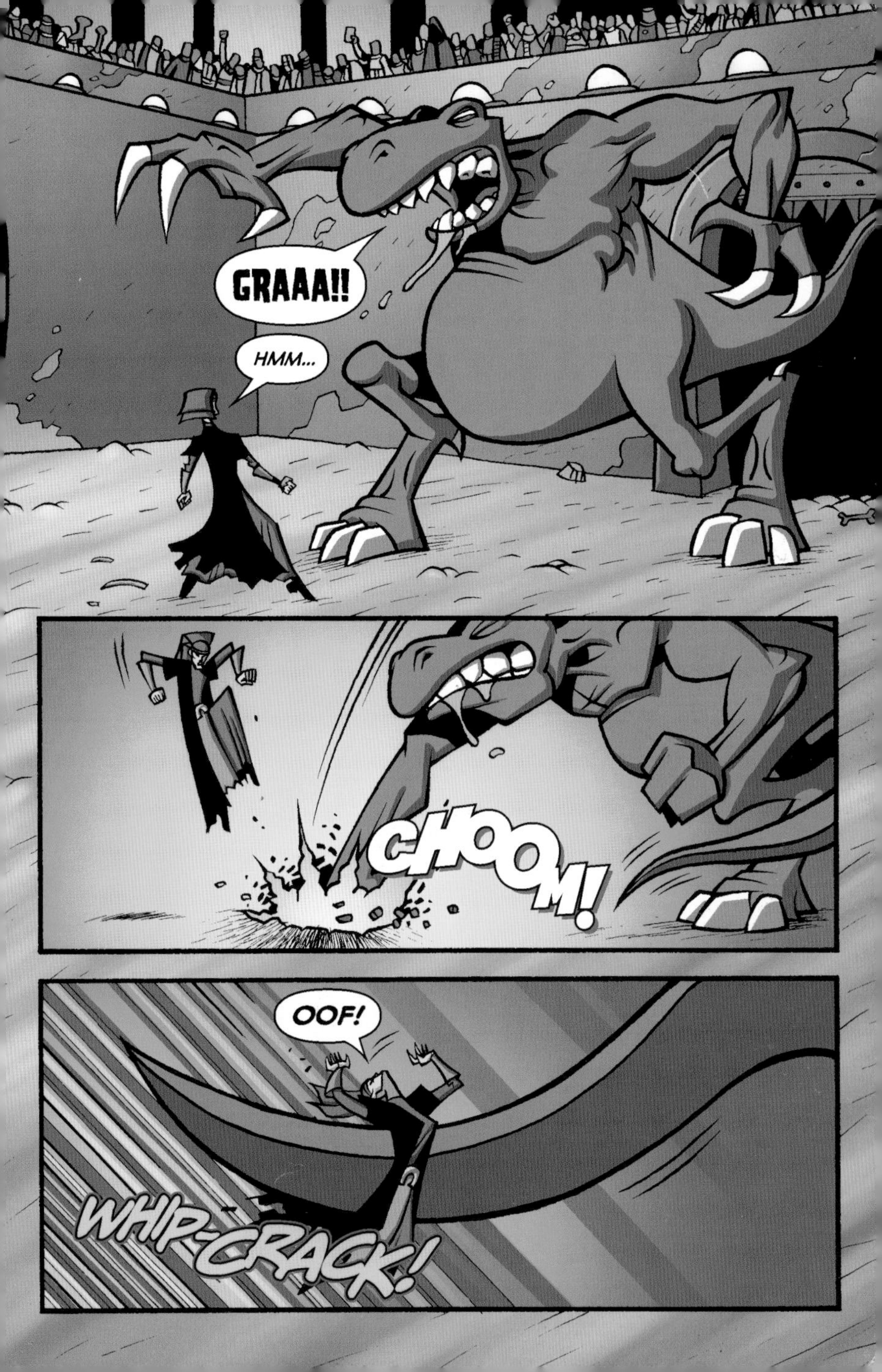
GRAAA!!
HMM...
CHOOOM!
OOF!
WHIP-CRACK!

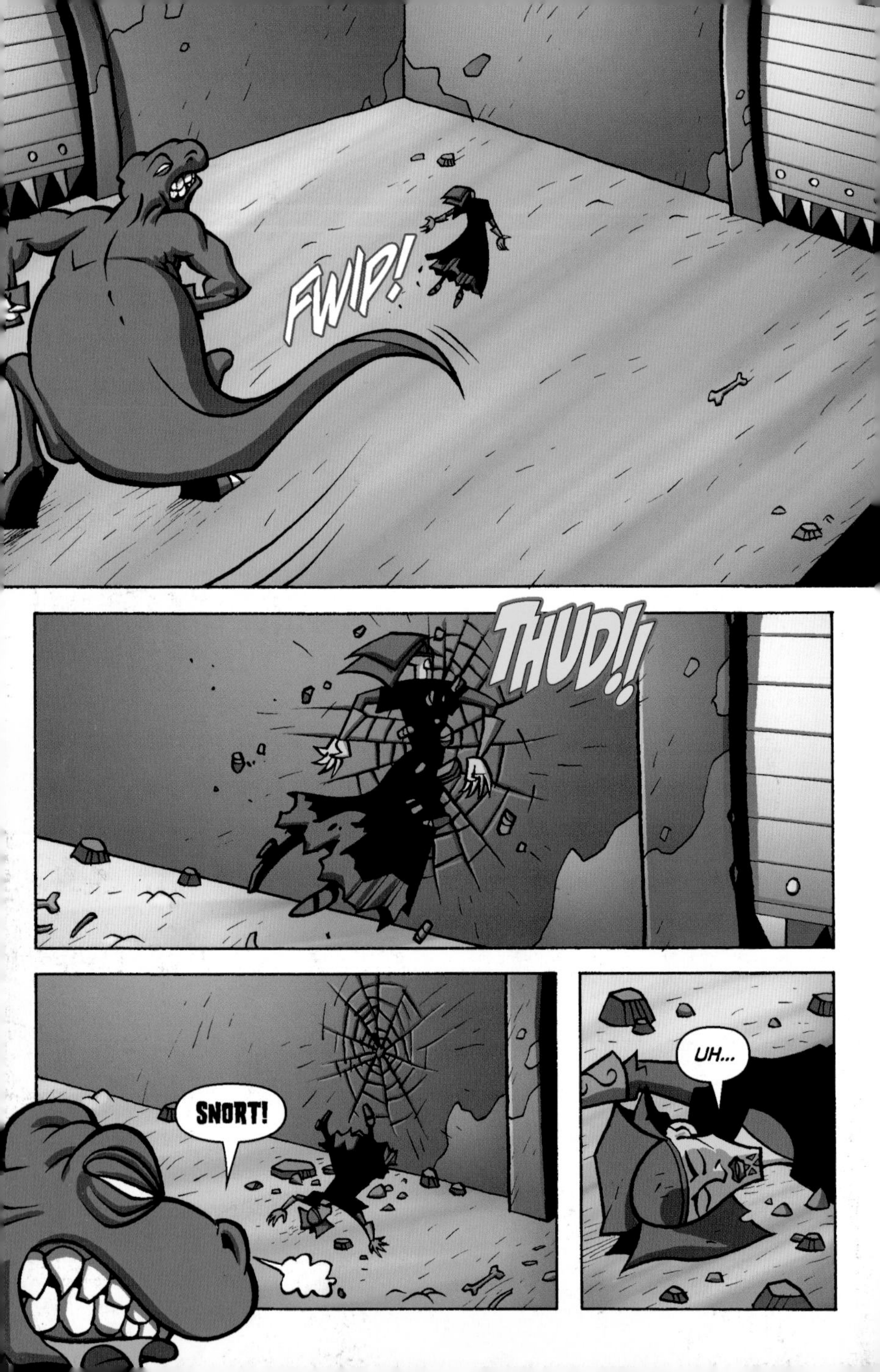
FWIP!
THUD!!
SNORT!
UH...

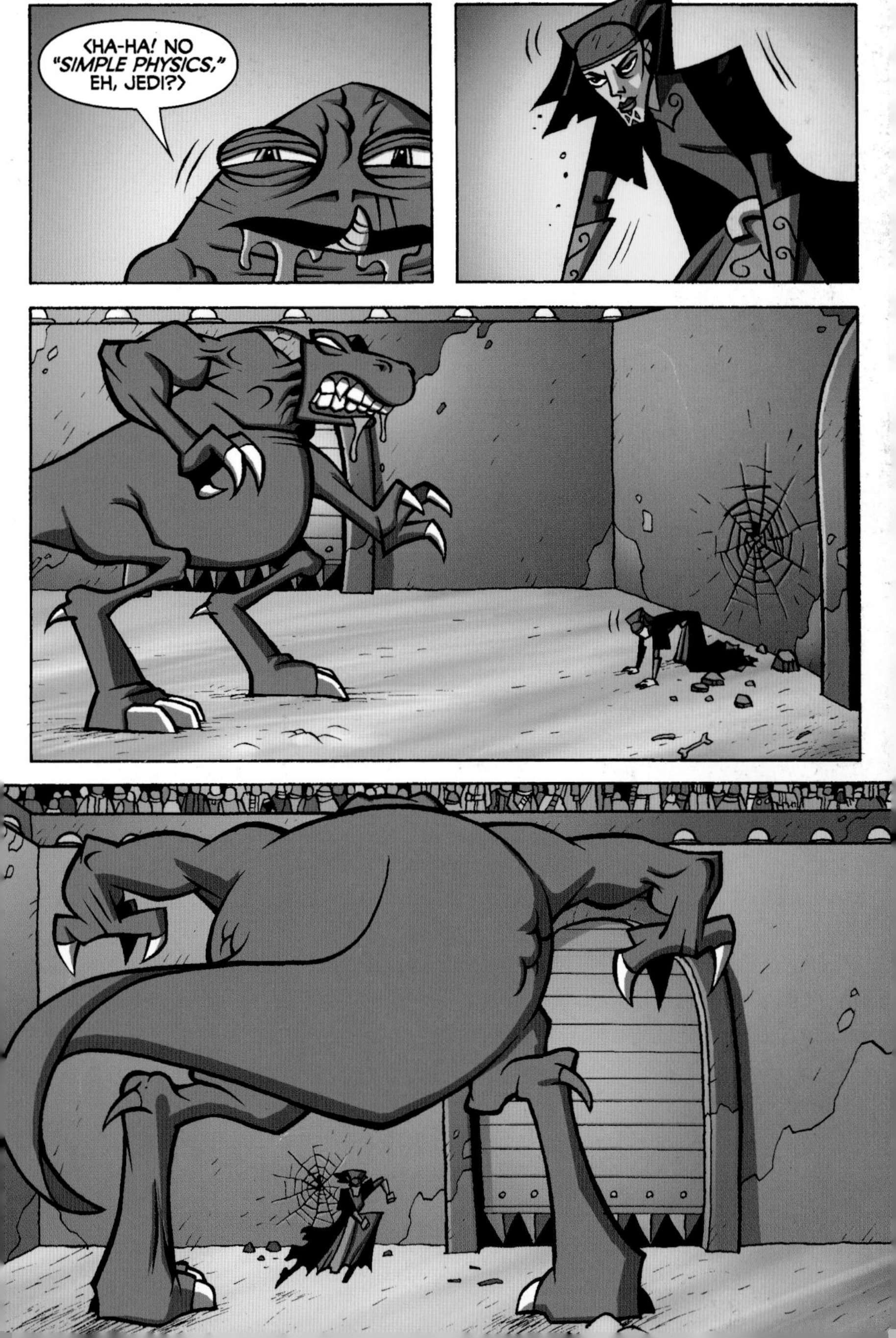
<HA-HA! NO "SIMPLE PHYSICS," EH, JEDI?>

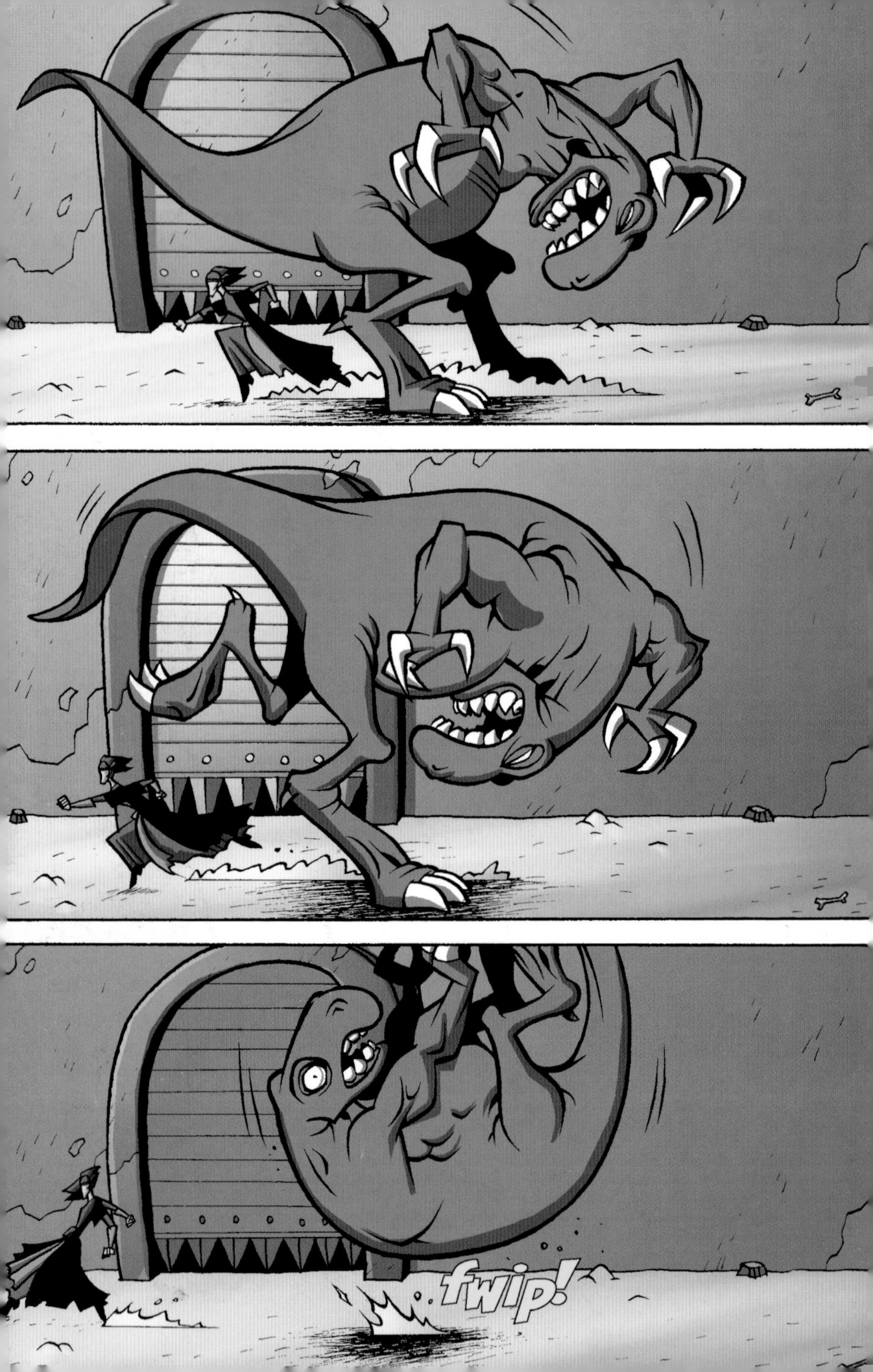
fwip!

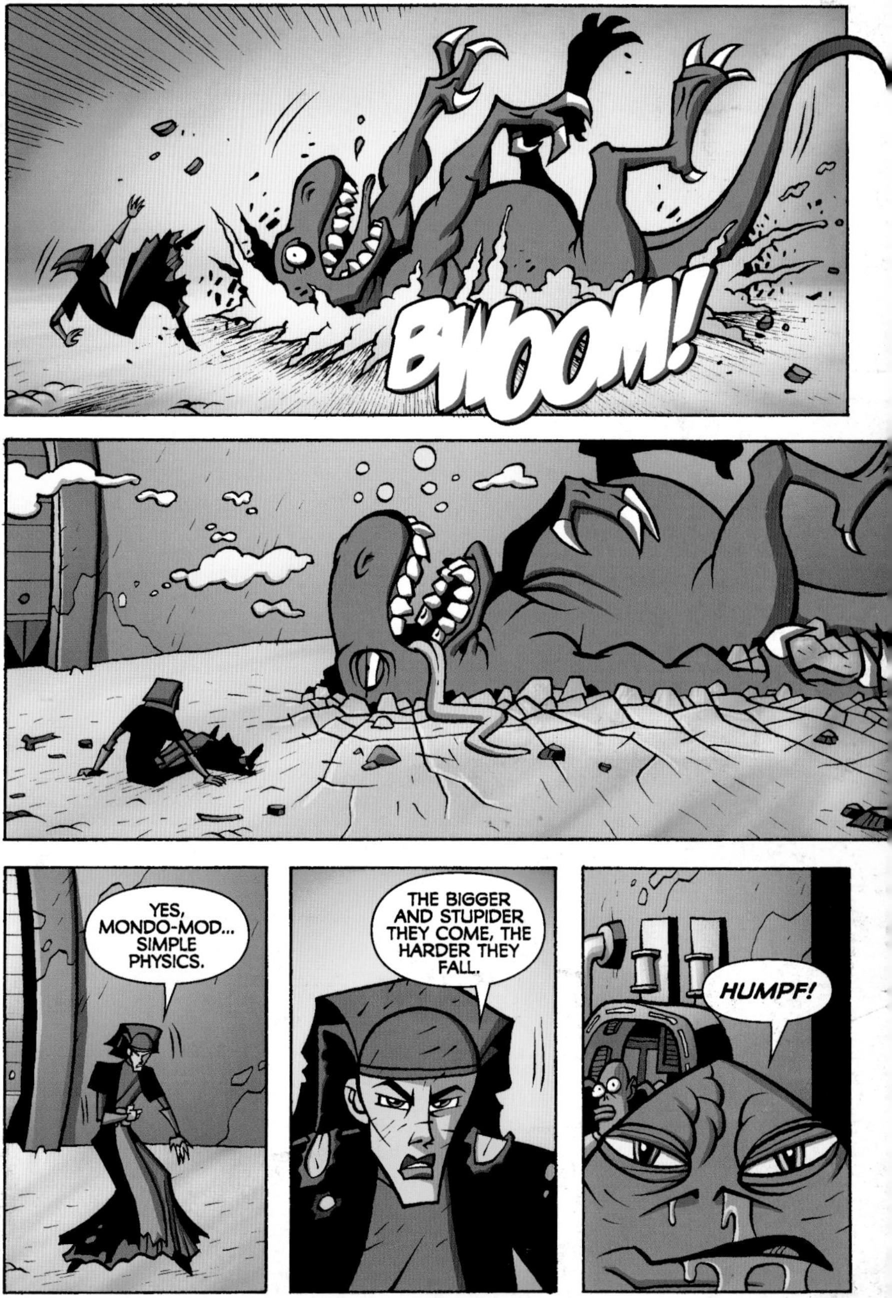
BWOOM!
YES, MONDO-MOD... SIMPLE PHYSICS.
THE BIGGER AND STUPIDER THEY COME, THE HARDER THEY FALL.
HUMPF!

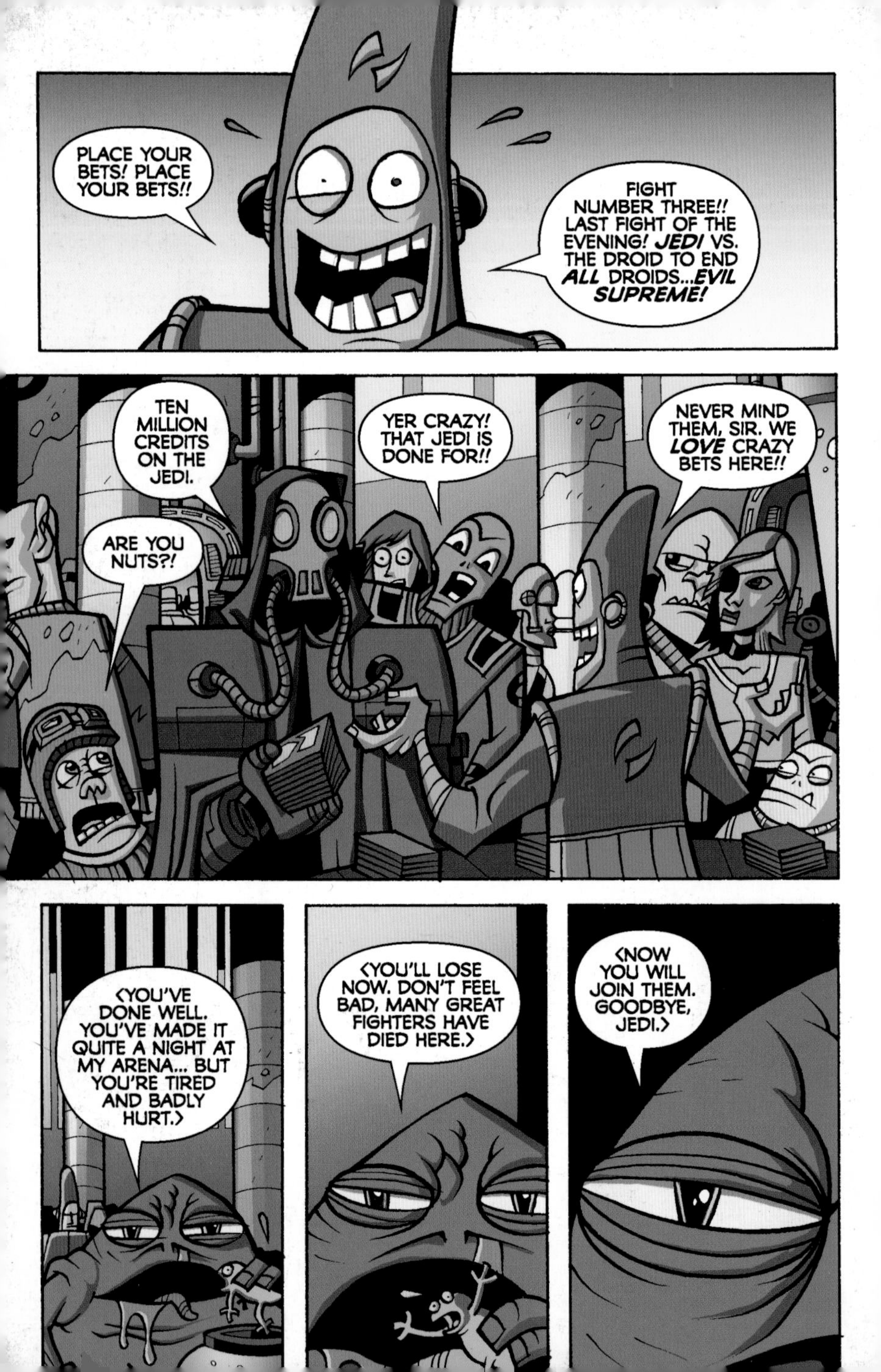
PLACE YOUR BETS! PLACE YOUR BETS!!
FIGHT NUMBER THREE!! LAST FIGHT OF THE EVENING! *JEDI* VS. THE DROID TO END *ALL* DROIDS...*EVIL SUPREME!*
TEN MILLION CREDITS ON THE JEDI.
ARE YOU NUTS?!
YER CRAZY! THAT JEDI IS DONE FOR!!
NEVER MIND THEM, SIR. WE *LOVE* CRAZY BETS HERE!!
<YOU'VE DONE WELL. YOU'VE MADE IT QUITE A NIGHT AT MY ARENA... BUT YOU'RE TIRED AND BADLY HURT.>
<YOU'LL LOSE NOW. DON'T FEEL BAD, MANY GREAT FIGHTERS HAVE DIED HERE.>
<NOW YOU WILL JOIN THEM. GOODBYE, JEDI.>

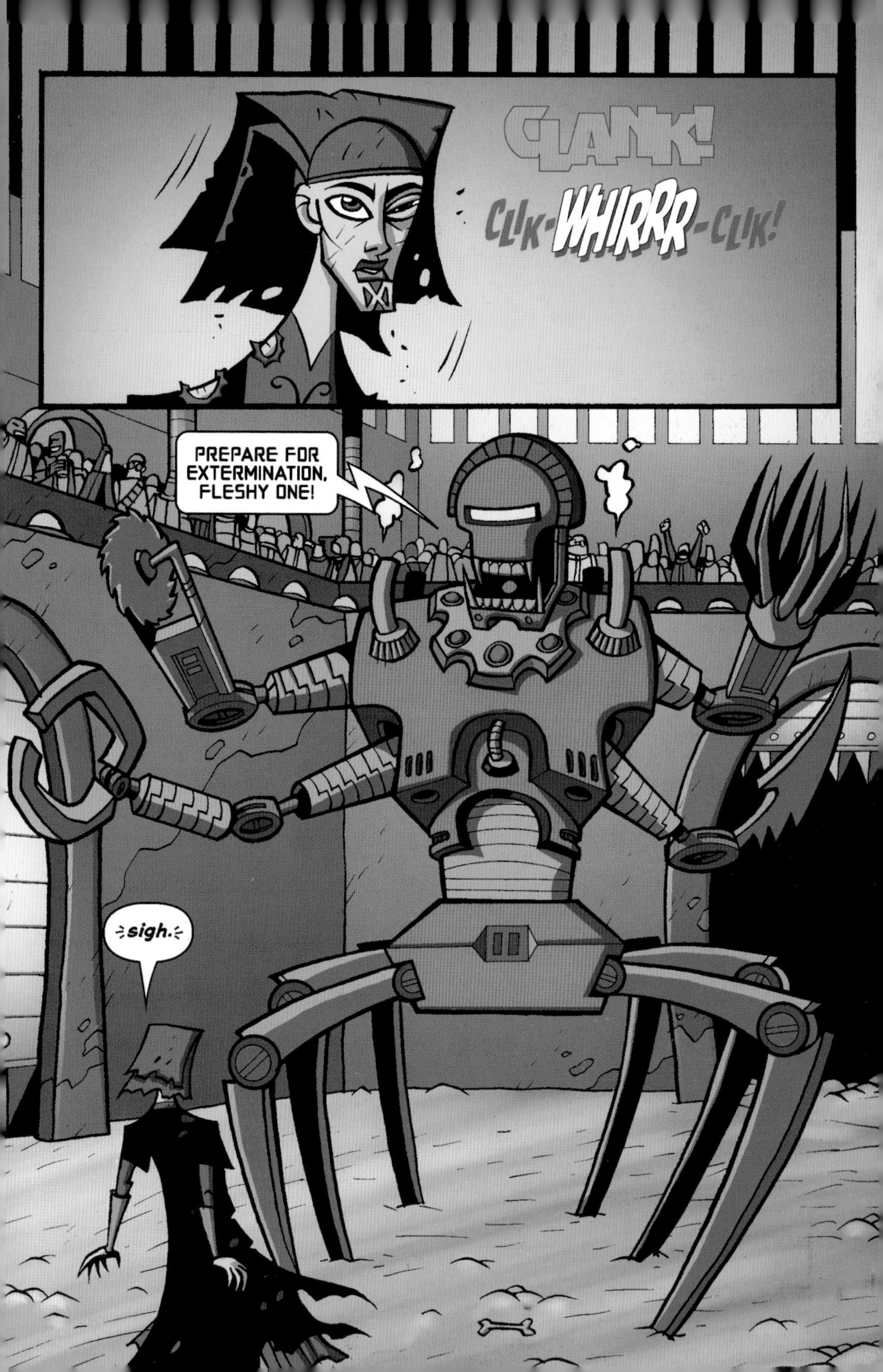
CLANK!
CLIK-WHIRRR-CLIK!
PREPARE FOR EXTERMINATION, FLESHY ONE!
sigh.

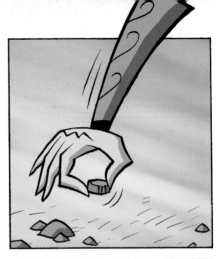

PAP!

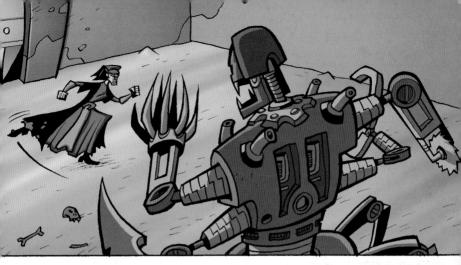

FWOOOSH!

KISH!

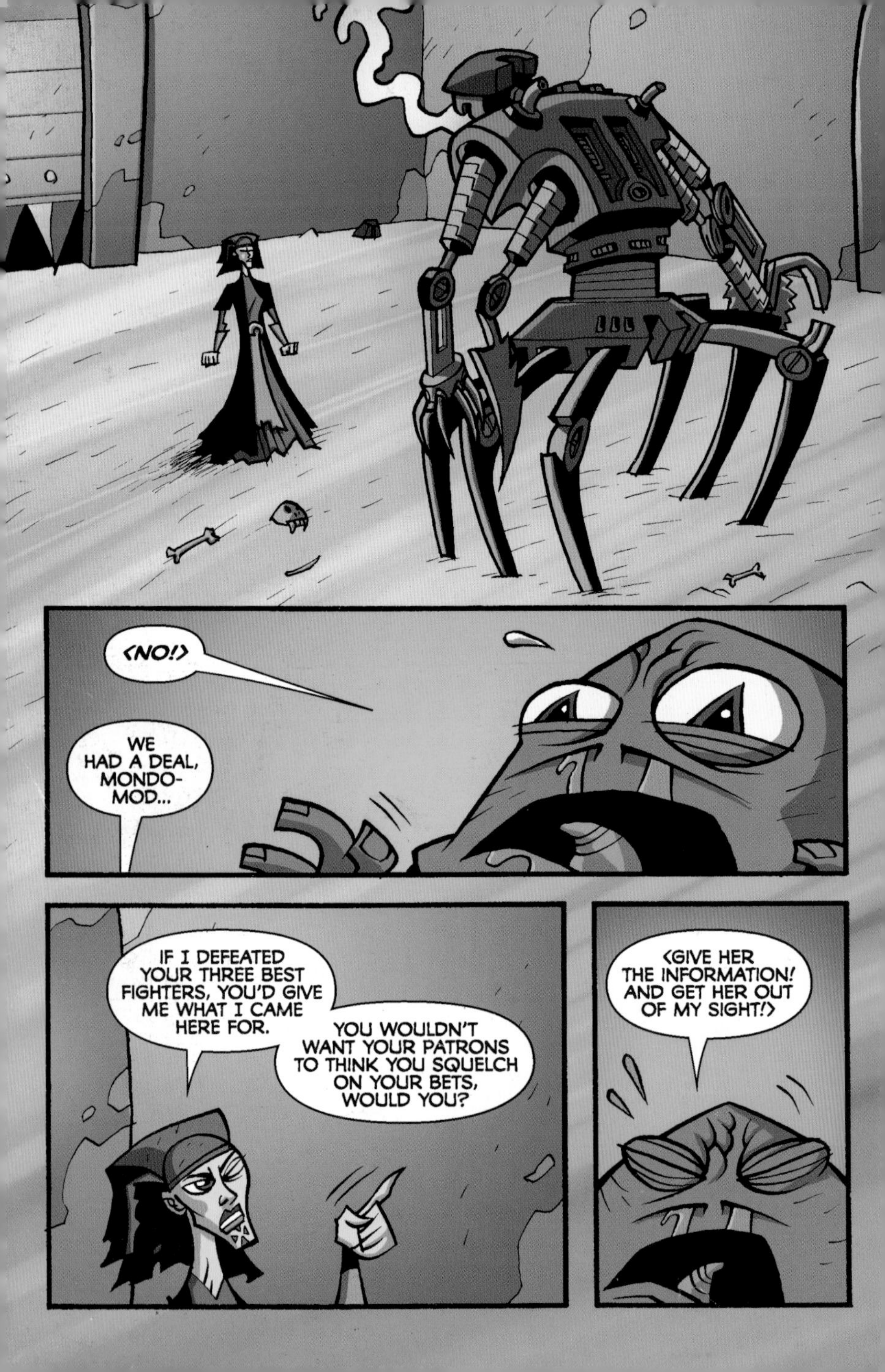
<NO!>
WE HAD A DEAL, MONDO-MOD...
IF I DEFEATED YOUR THREE BEST FIGHTERS, YOU'D GIVE ME WHAT I CAME HERE FOR.
YOU WOULDN'T WANT YOUR PATRONS TO THINK YOU SQUELCH ON YOUR BETS, WOULD YOU?
<GIVE HER THE INFORMATION! AND GET HER OUT OF MY SIGHT!>

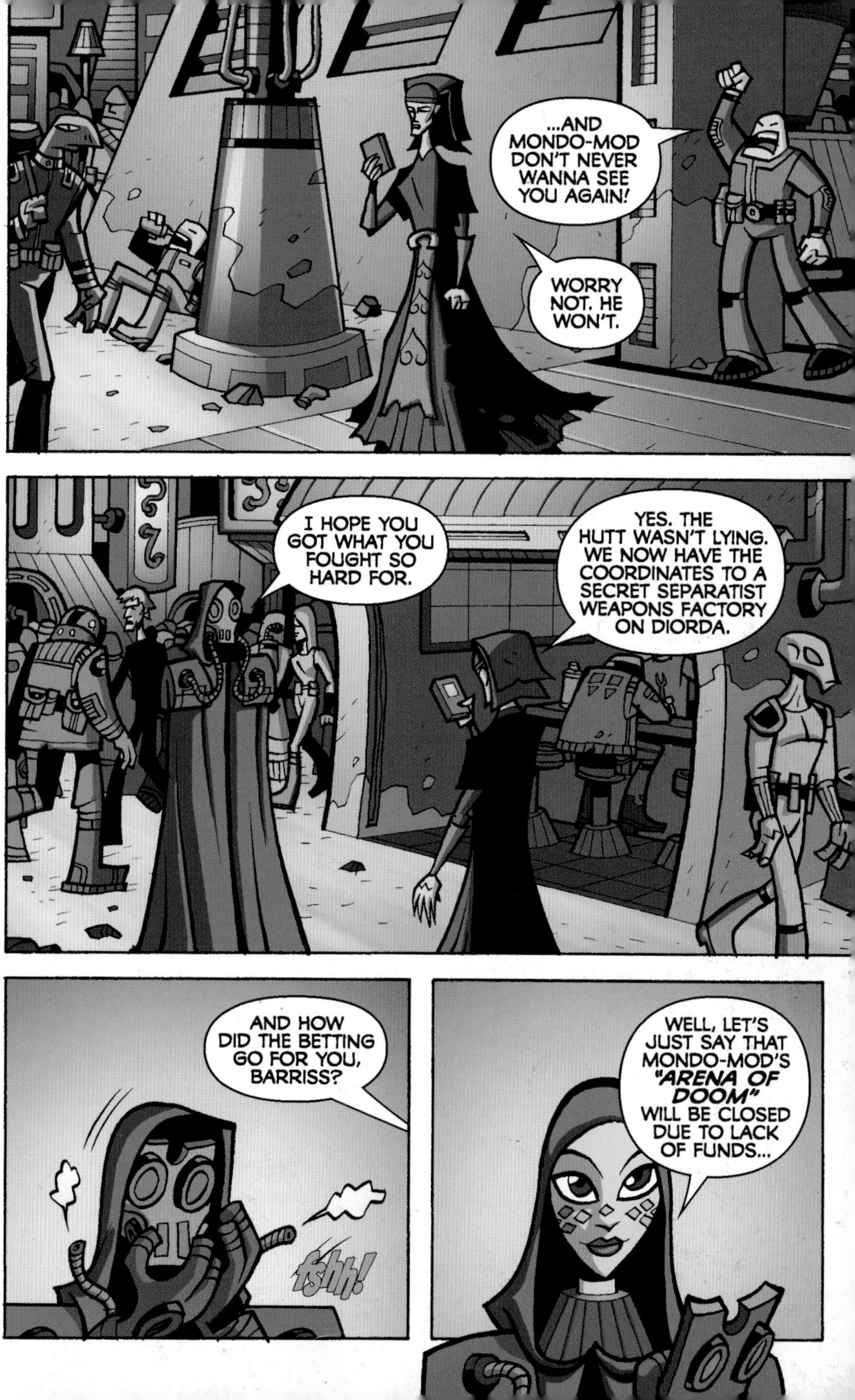
...AND MONDO-MOD DON'T NEVER WANNA SEE YOU AGAIN!
WORRY NOT. HE WON'T.
I HOPE YOU GOT WHAT YOU FOUGHT SO HARD FOR.
YES. THE HUTT WASN'T LYING. WE NOW HAVE THE COORDINATES TO A SECRET SEPARATIST WEAPONS FACTORY ON DIORDA.
AND HOW DID THE BETTING GO FOR YOU, BARRISS?
fshh!
WELL, LET'S JUST SAY THAT MONDO-MOD'S *"ARENA OF DOOM"* WILL BE CLOSED DUE TO LACK OF FUNDS...

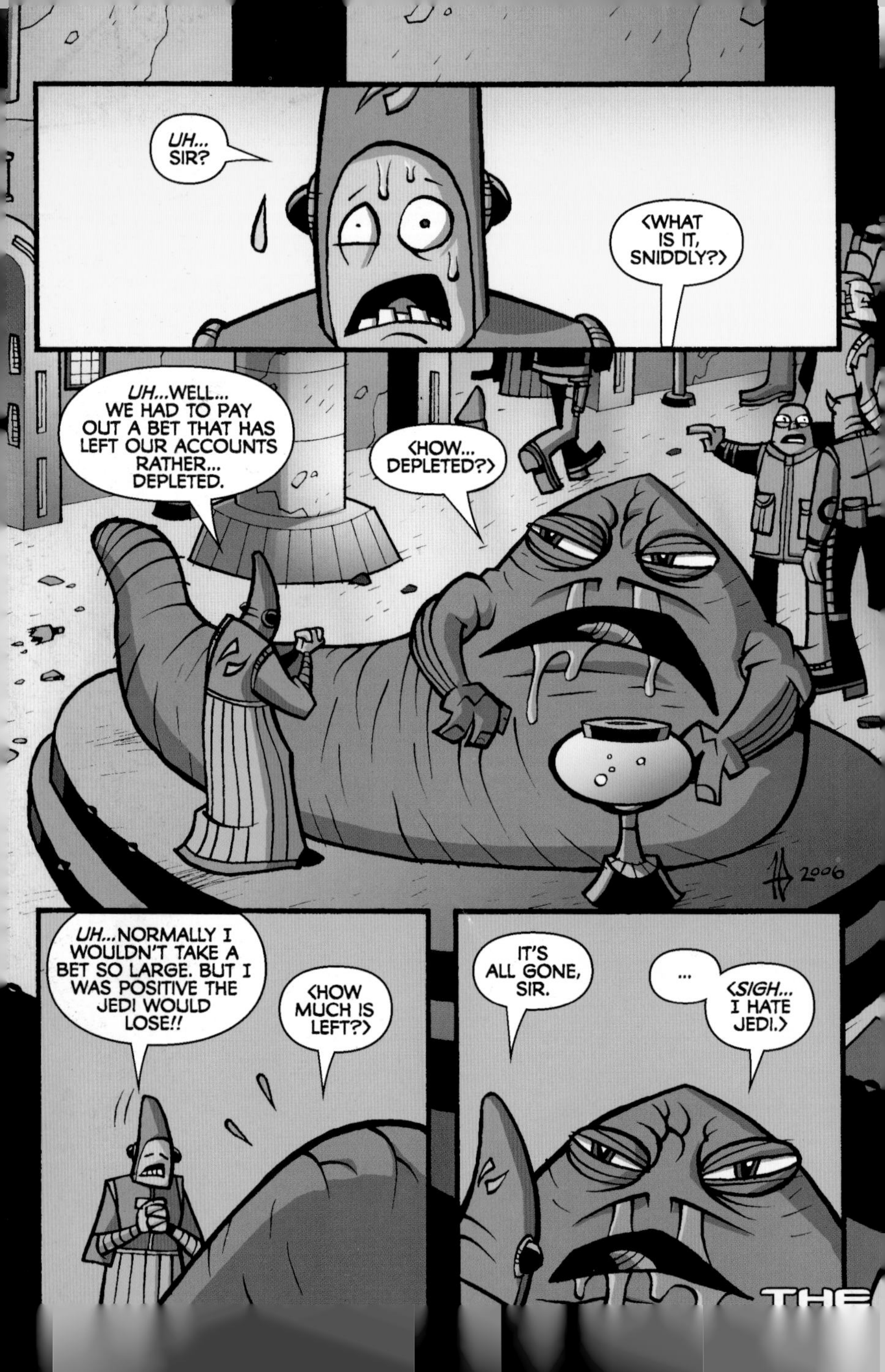
UH... SIR?
<WHAT IS IT, SNIDDLY?>
UH...WELL... WE HAD TO PAY OUT A BET THAT HAS LEFT OUR ACCOUNTS RATHER... DEPLETED.
<HOW... DEPLETED?>
UH...NORMALLY I WOULDN'T TAKE A BET SO LARGE. BUT I WAS POSITIVE THE JEDI WOULD LOSE!!
<HOW MUCH IS LEFT?>
IT'S ALL GONE, SIR.
...
<SIGH... I HATE JEDI.>
THE

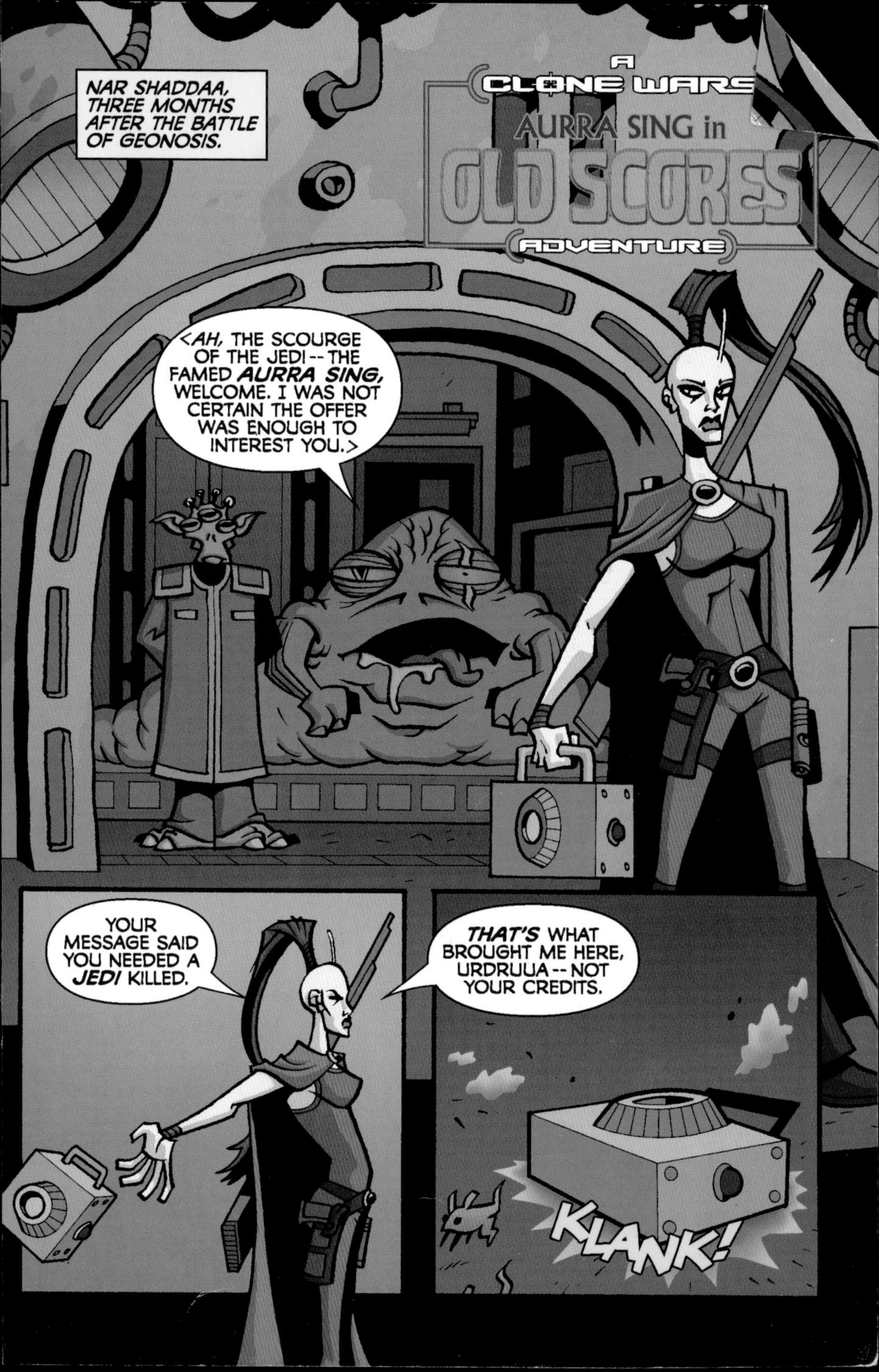
A CLONE WARS
AURRA SING in
OLD SCORES
ADVENTURE
NAR SHADDAA, THREE MONTHS AFTER THE BATTLE OF GEONOSIS.
<AH, THE SCOURGE OF THE JEDI -- THE FAMED AURRA SING, WELCOME. I WAS NOT CERTAIN THE OFFER WAS ENOUGH TO INTEREST YOU.>
YOUR MESSAGE SAID YOU NEEDED A JEDI KILLED.
THAT'S WHAT BROUGHT ME HERE, URDRUUA -- NOT YOUR CREDITS.
KLANK!

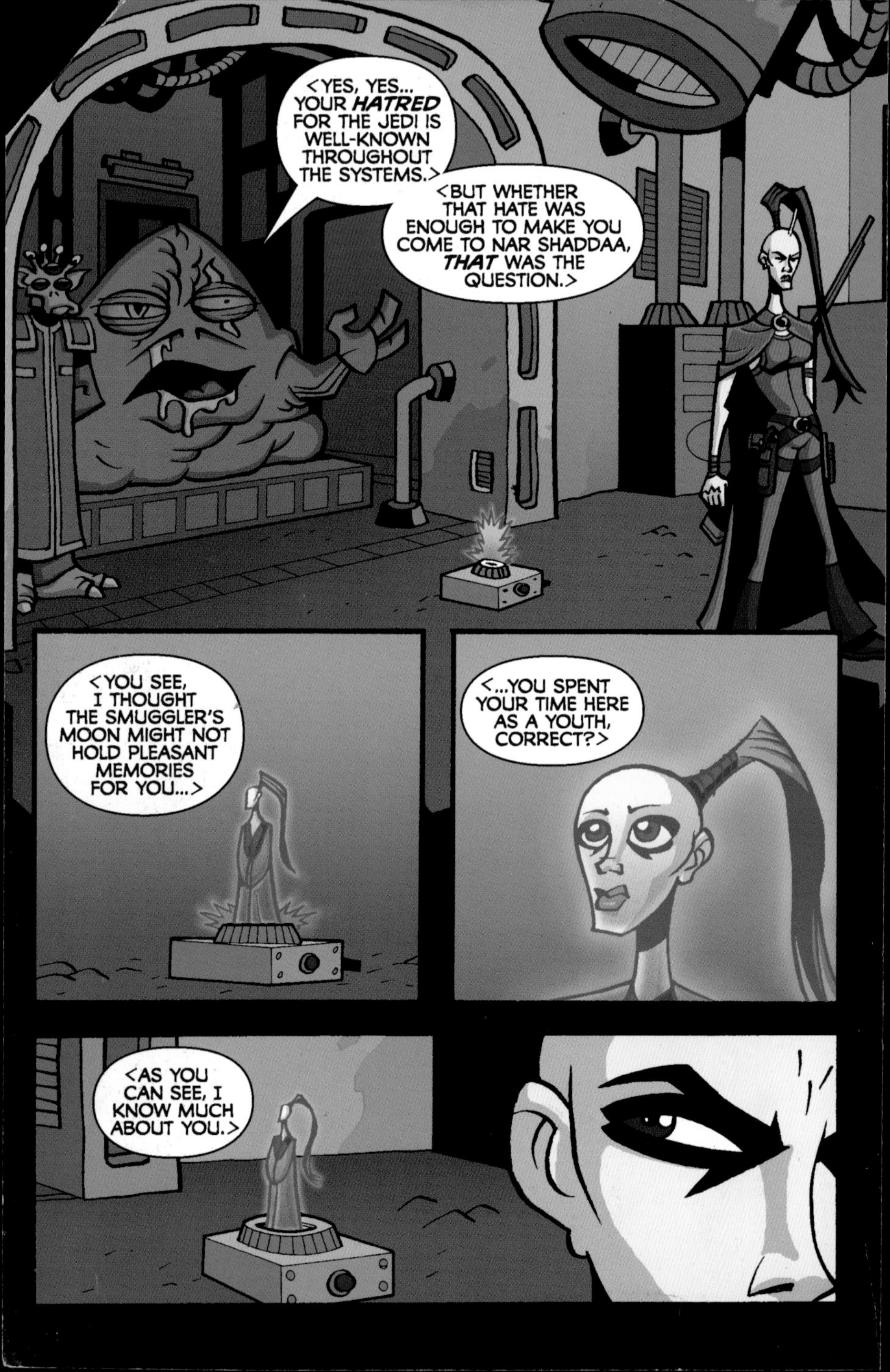
<YES, YES... YOUR **HATRED** FOR THE JEDI IS WELL-KNOWN THROUGHOUT THE SYSTEMS.>
<BUT WHETHER THAT HATE WAS ENOUGH TO MAKE YOU COME TO NAR SHADDAA, ***THAT*** WAS THE QUESTION.>
<YOU SEE, I THOUGHT THE SMUGGLER'S MOON MIGHT NOT HOLD PLEASANT MEMORIES FOR YOU...>
<...YOU SPENT YOUR TIME HERE AS A YOUTH, CORRECT?>
<AS YOU CAN SEE, I KNOW MUCH ABOUT YOU.>

<FROM THE TEMPLE OF THE JEDI...>
<...TO YOUR RETURN TO NAR SHADDAA, WHERE YOU *CONTINUED* YOUR TRAINING AT THE EXPENSE OF THE HUTTS.>
<YOU TURNED ON BOTH OF YOUR MASTERS...NOT CONSIDERATE, NOT AT ALL.>
<SOME WOULD SAY... ***UNGRATEFUL.***>

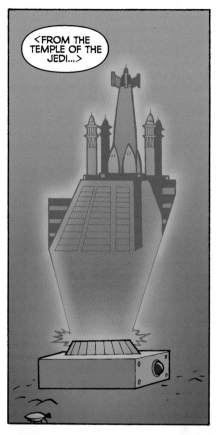

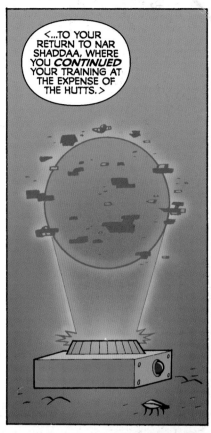

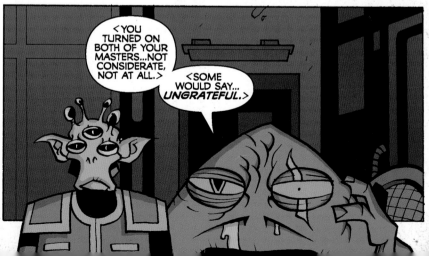

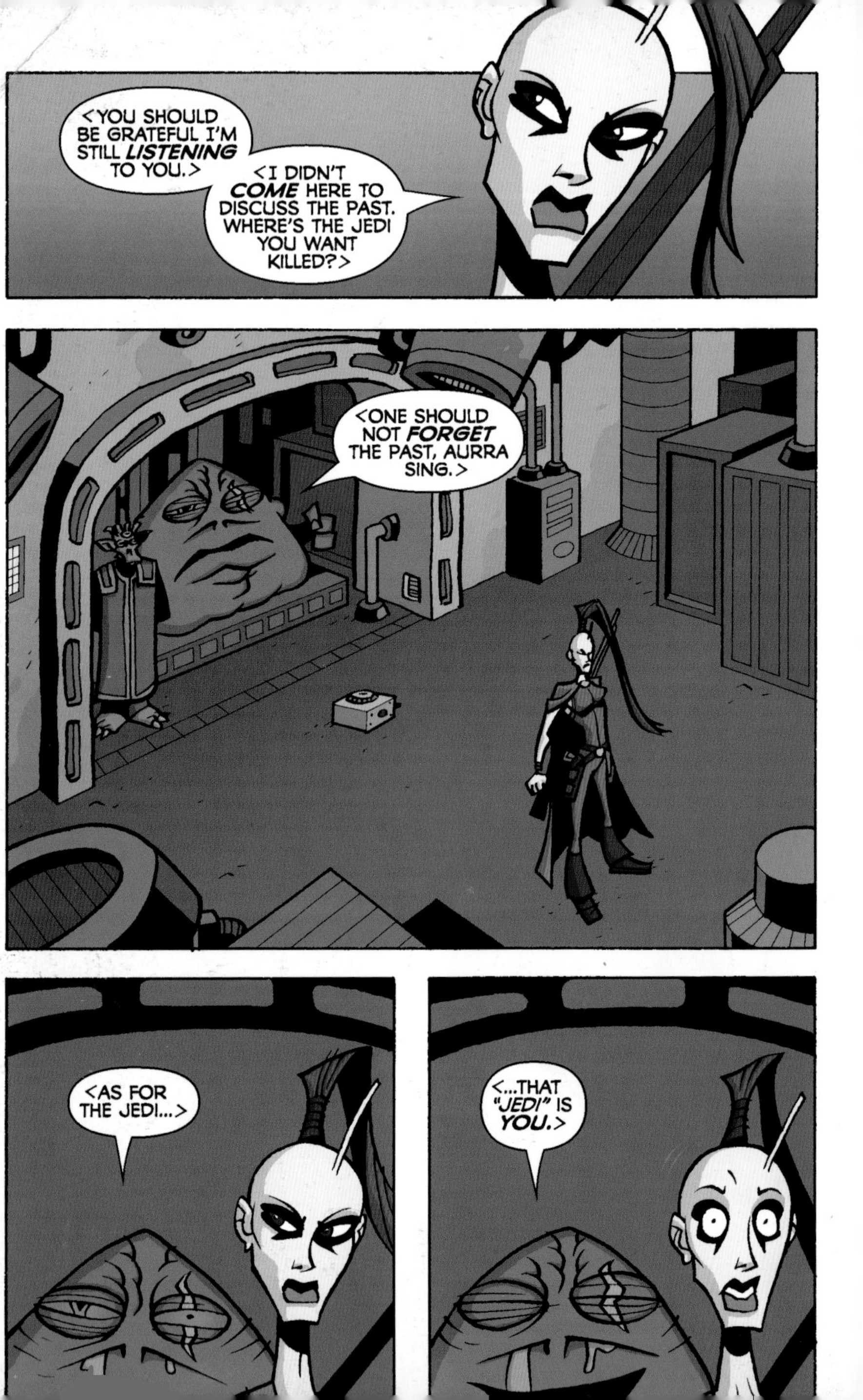
<YOU SHOULD BE GRATEFUL I'M STILL *LISTENING* TO YOU.>
<I DIDN'T *COME* HERE TO DISCUSS THE PAST. WHERE'S THE JEDI YOU WANT KILLED?>
<ONE SHOULD NOT *FORGET* THE PAST, AURRA SING.>
<AS FOR THE JEDI...>
<...THAT *"JEDI"* IS *YOU.*>

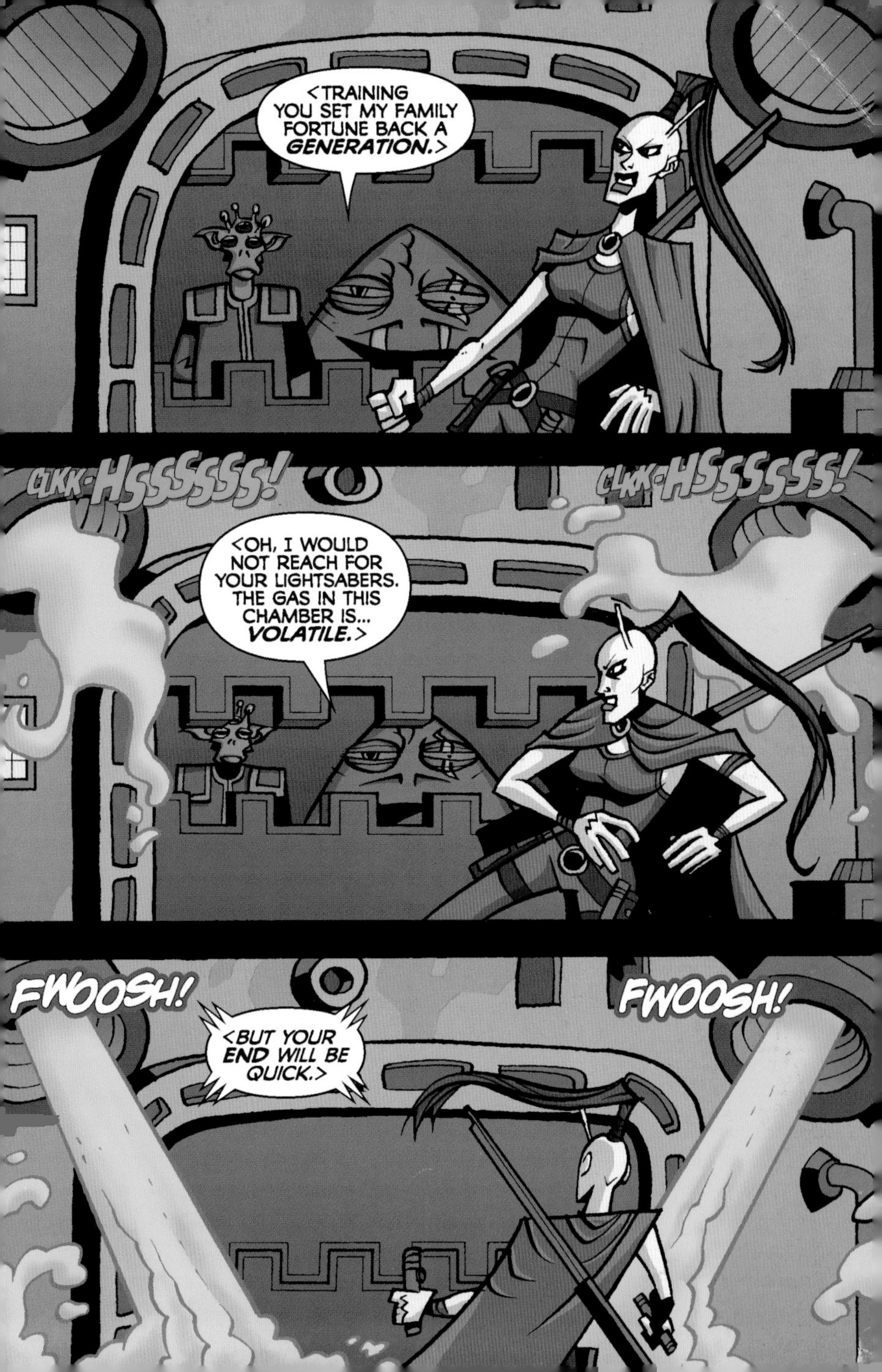

<TRAINING YOU SET MY FAMILY FORTUNE BACK A *GENERATION.*>
CLKK-HSSSSSSS!
CLKK-HSSSSSS!
<OH, I WOULD NOT REACH FOR YOUR LIGHTSABERS. THE GAS IN THIS CHAMBER IS... *VOLATILE.*>
FWOOSH!
FWOOSH!
<*BUT YOUR* ***END*** *WILL BE QUICK.*>

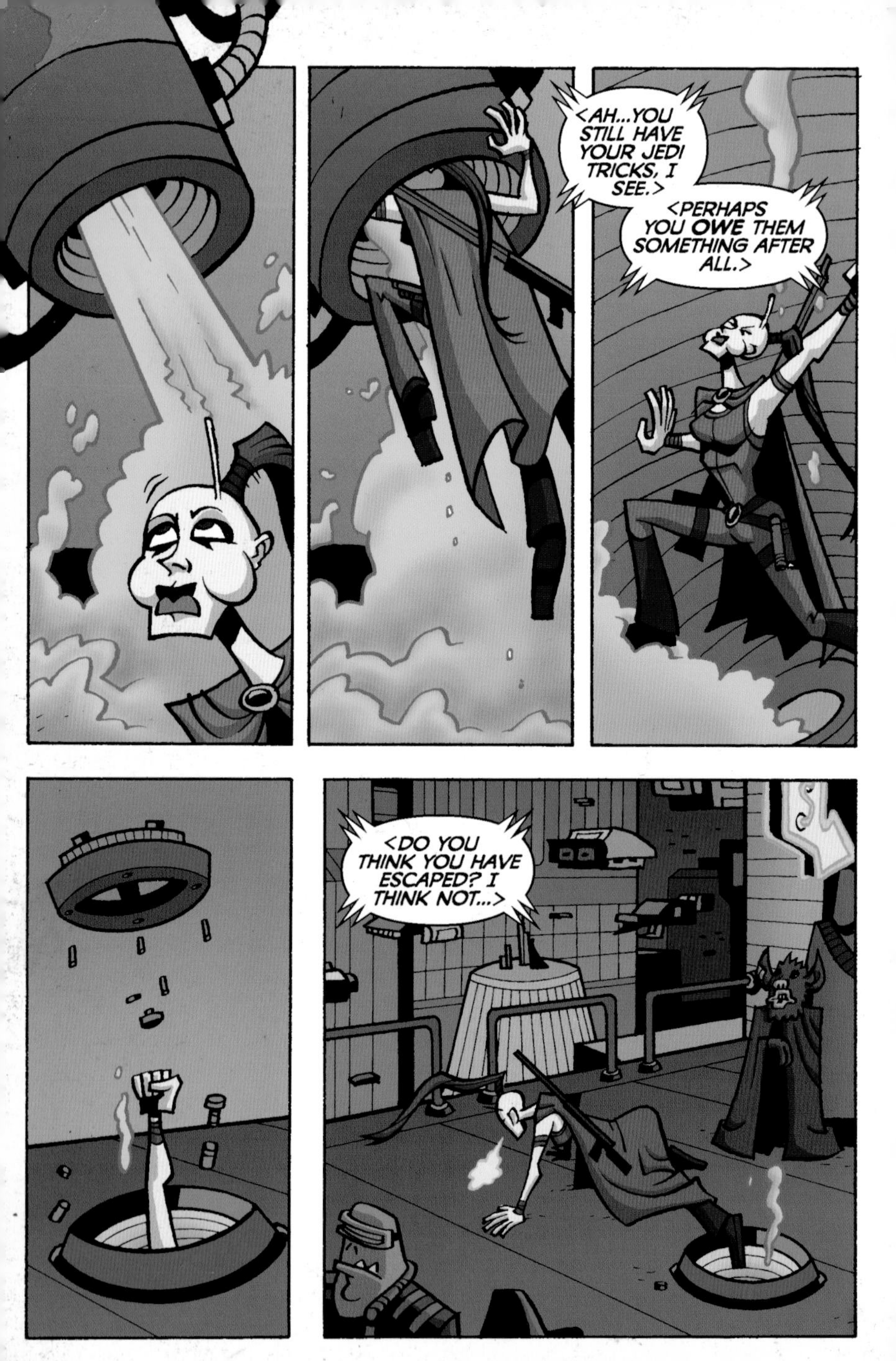
<AH...YOU STILL HAVE YOUR JEDI TRICKS, I SEE.>
<PERHAPS YOU **OWE** THEM SOMETHING AFTER ALL.>
<DO YOU THINK YOU HAVE ESCAPED? I THINK NOT...>

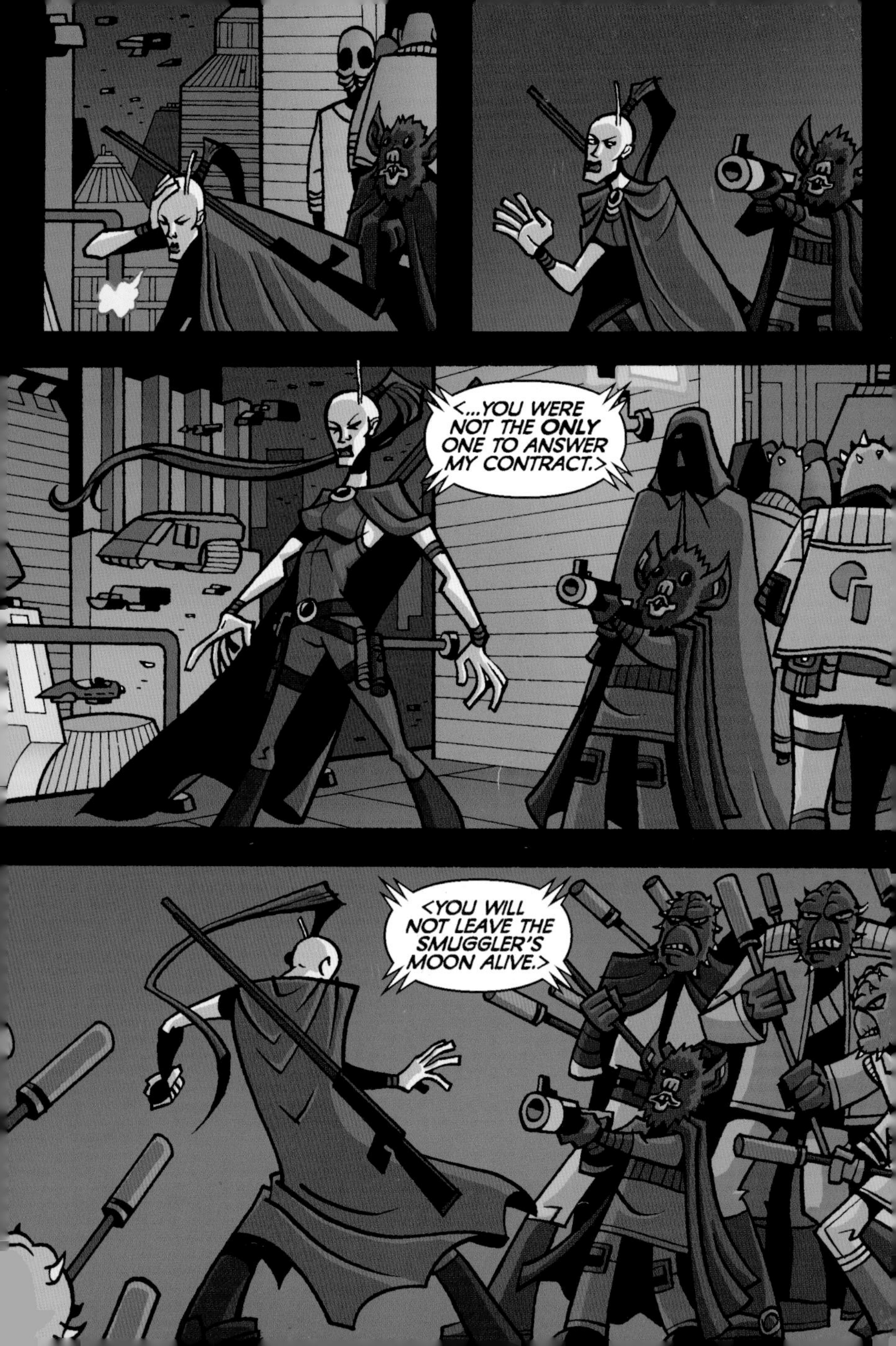
<...YOU WERE NOT THE ONLY ONE TO ANSWER MY CONTRACT.>
<YOU WILL NOT LEAVE THE SMUGGLER'S MOON ALIVE.>

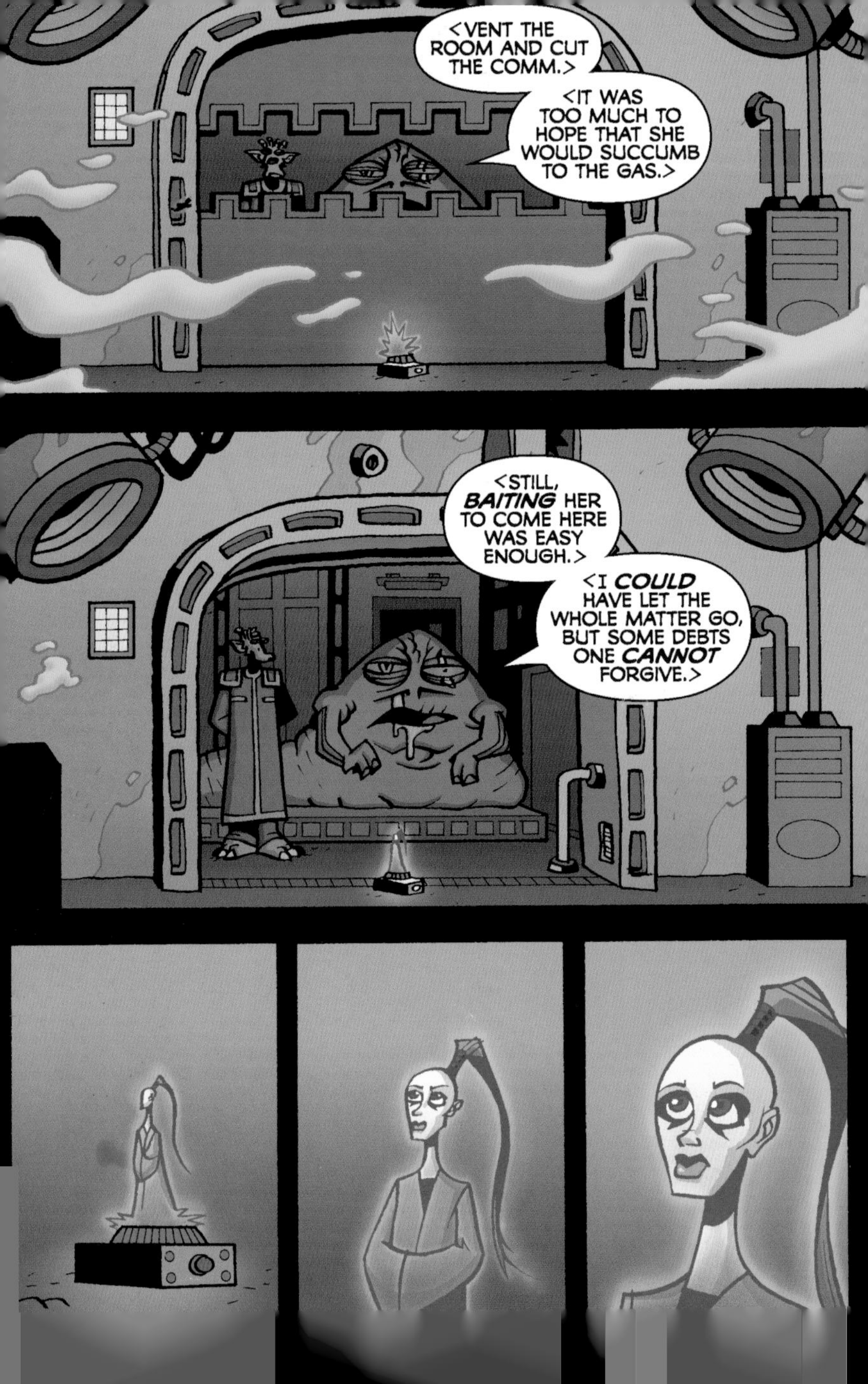
<VENT THE ROOM AND CUT THE COMM.>
<IT WAS TOO MUCH TO HOPE THAT SHE WOULD SUCCUMB TO THE GAS.>
<STILL, BAITING HER TO COME HERE WAS EASY ENOUGH.>
<I COULD HAVE LET THE WHOLE MATTER GO, BUT SOME DEBTS ONE CANNOT FORGIVE.>

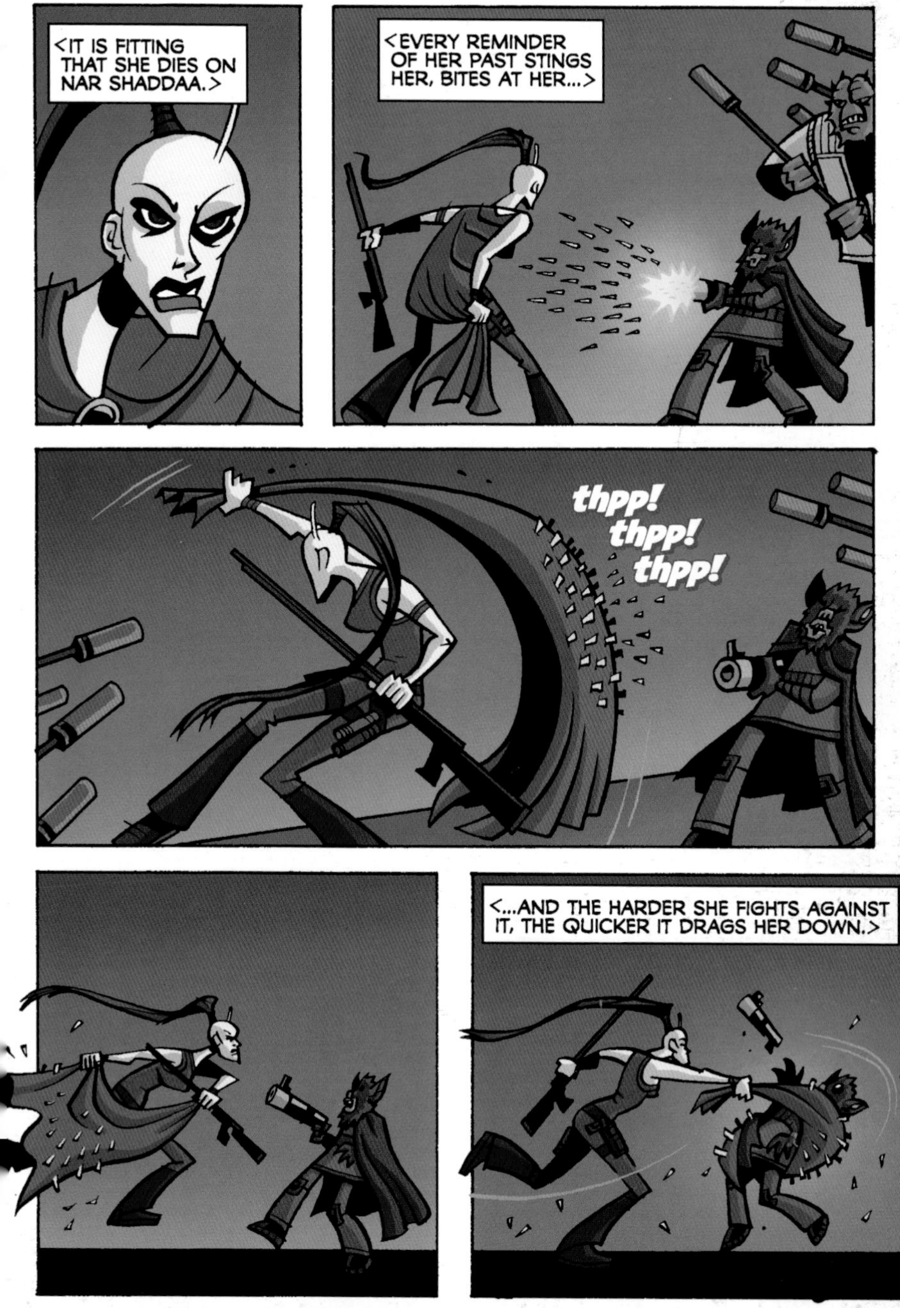
<IT IS FITTING THAT SHE DIES ON NAR SHADDAA.>
<EVERY REMINDER OF HER PAST STINGS HER, BITES AT HER...>
thpp! thpp! thpp!
<...AND THE HARDER SHE FIGHTS AGAINST IT, THE QUICKER IT DRAGS HER DOWN.>

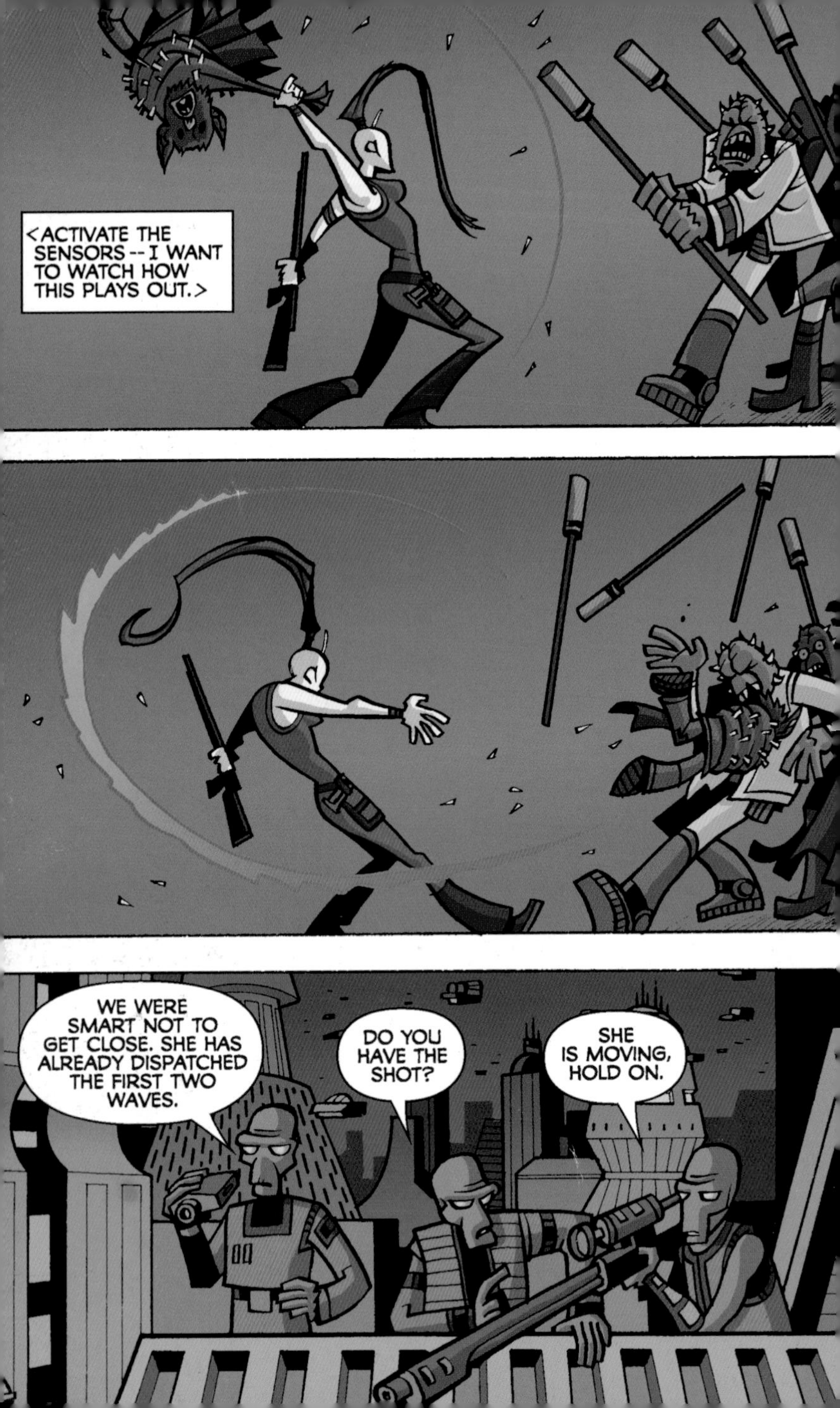
<ACTIVATE THE SENSORS -- I WANT TO WATCH HOW THIS PLAYS OUT.>
WE WERE SMART NOT TO GET CLOSE. SHE HAS ALREADY DISPATCHED THE FIRST TWO WAVES.
DO YOU HAVE THE SHOT?
SHE IS MOVING, HOLD ON.

WAIT, I HAVE HER!

I JUST NEED TO ADJUST THE SC--

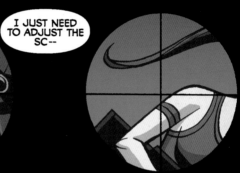

AIGH! SHE'S --

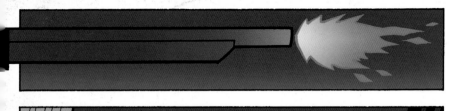

KA-BOOM!!

AMATEURS.

NEED SOME DISTANCE.

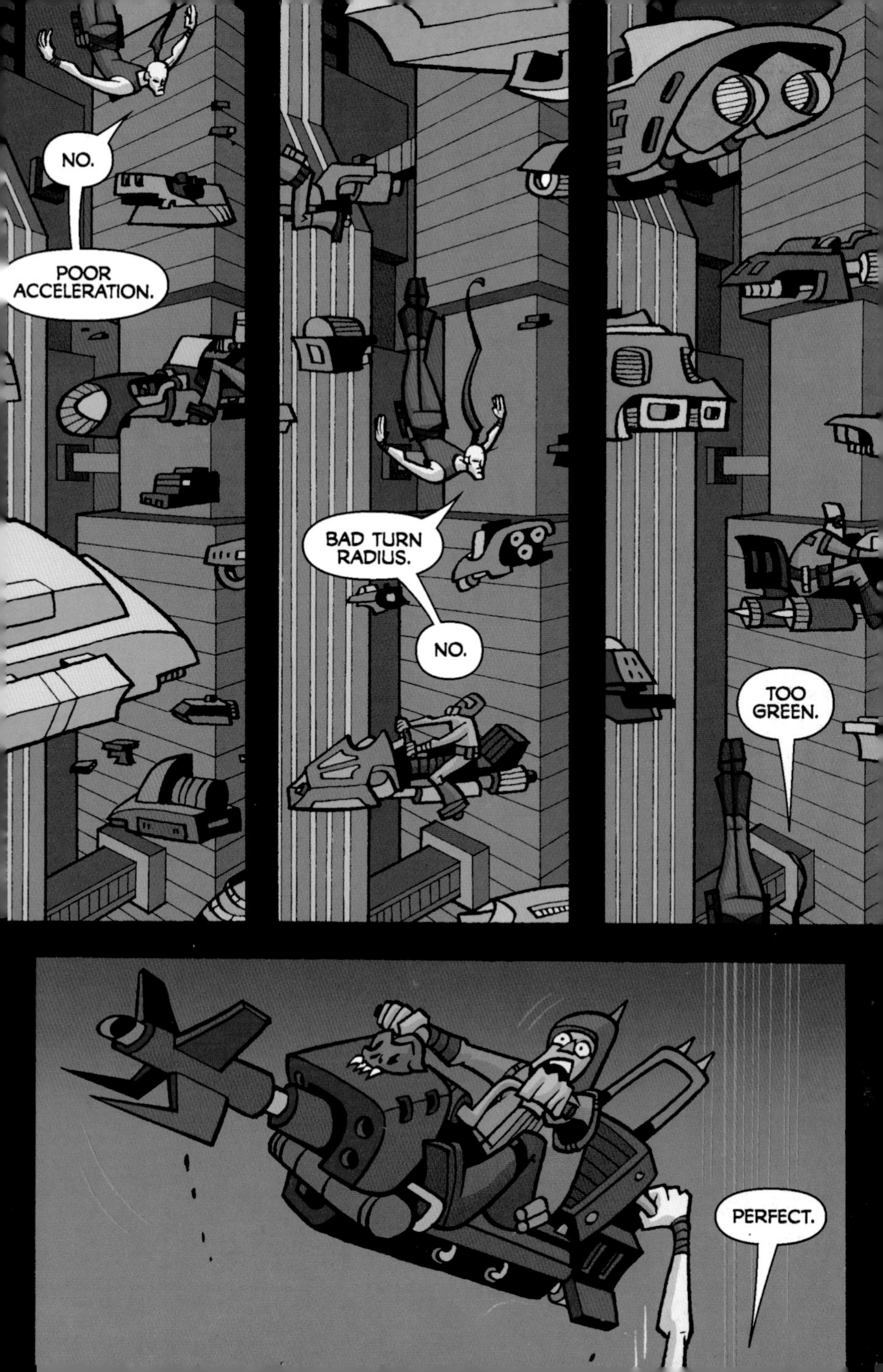
NO.
POOR ACCELERATION.
BAD TURN RADIUS.
NO.
TOO GREEN.
PERFECT.

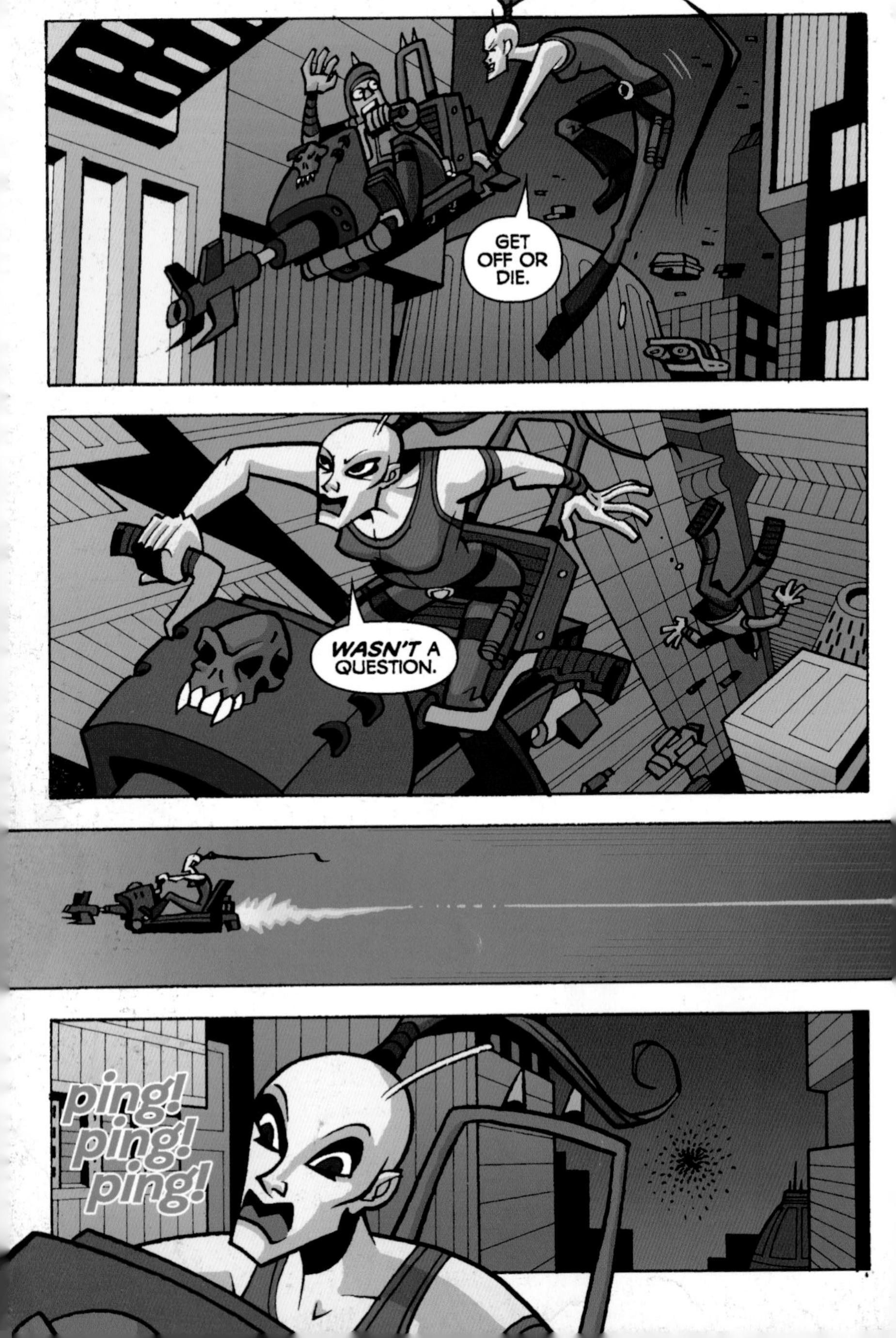
GET OFF OR DIE.
WASN'T A QUESTION.
ping! ping! ping!

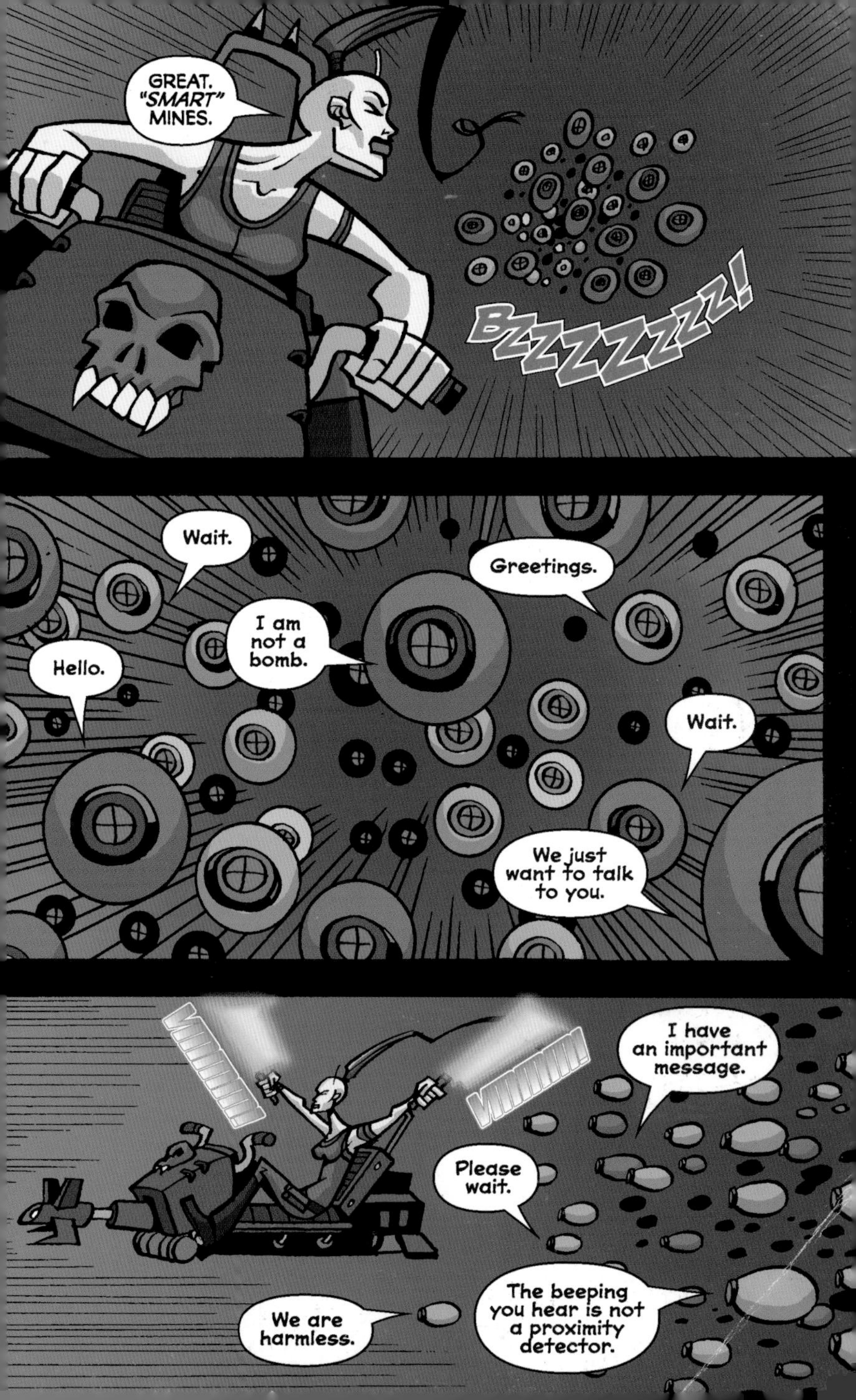
GREAT. "SMART" MINES.
BZZZZZZZ!
Wait.
Greetings.
I am not a bomb.
Hello.
Wait.
We just want to talk to you.
I have an important message.
Please wait.
We are harmless.
The beeping you hear is not a proximity detector.

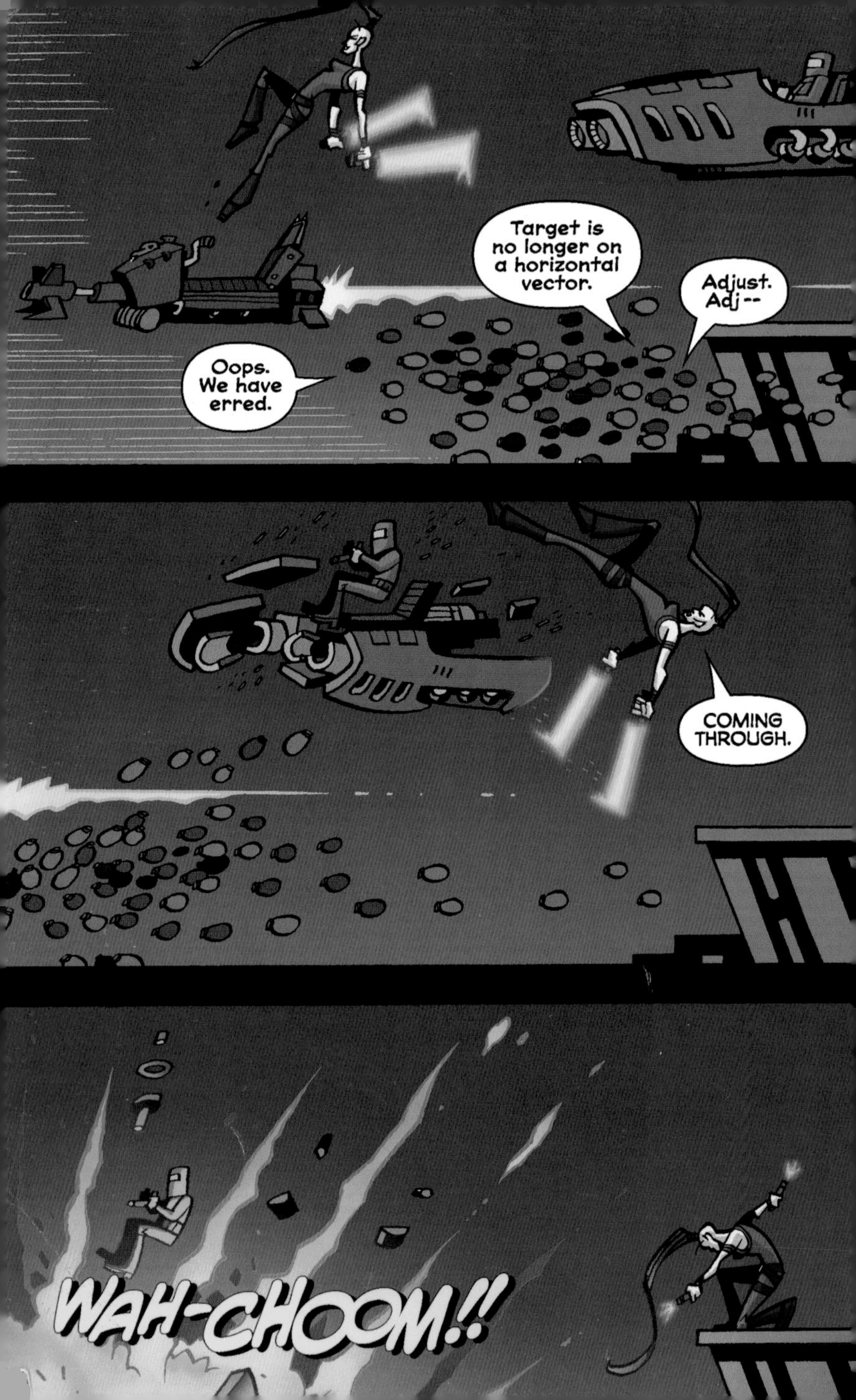
Target is no longer on a horizontal vector.
Adjust. Adj--
Oops. We have erred.
COMING THROUGH.
WAH-CHOOM!!

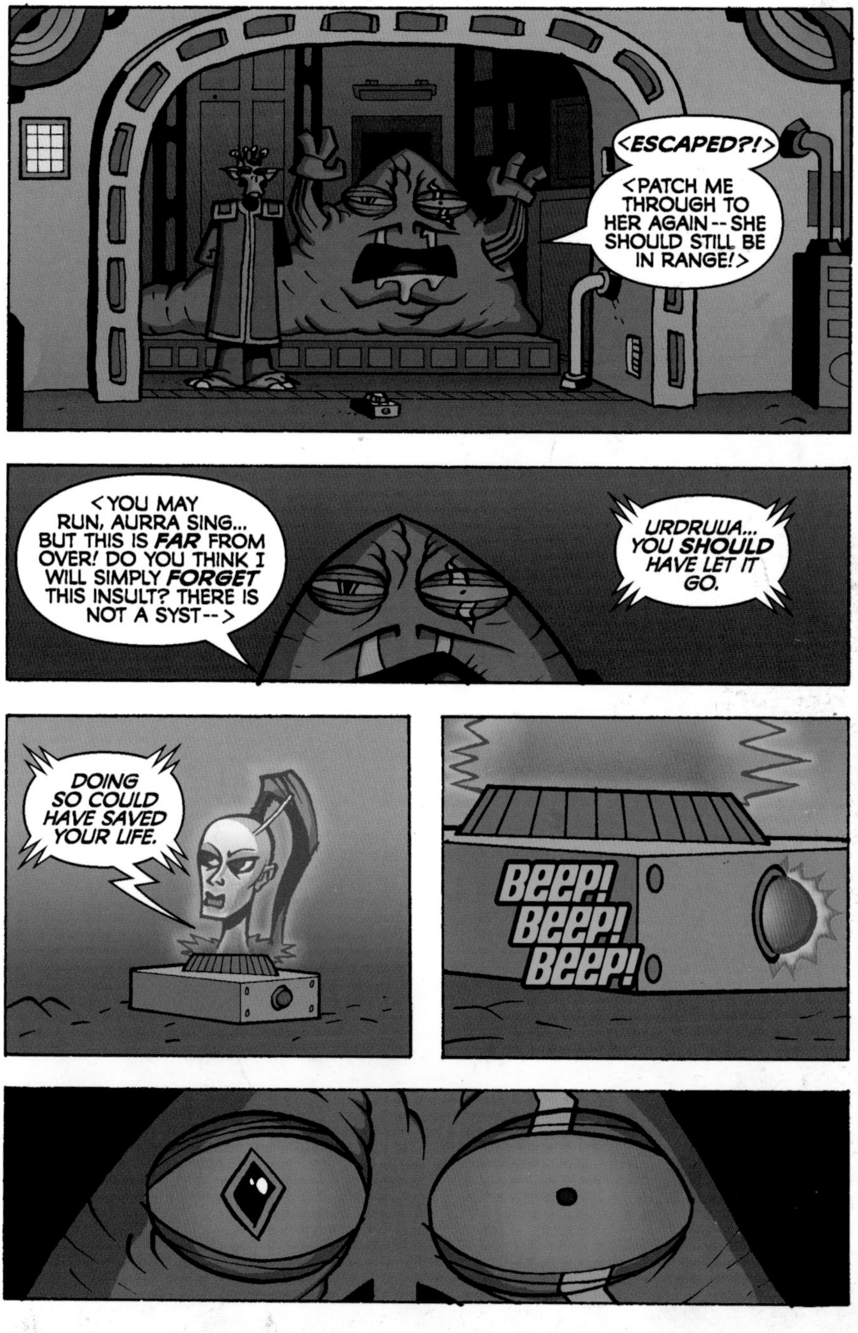

<ESCAPED?!>
<PATCH ME THROUGH TO HER AGAIN--SHE SHOULD STILL BE IN RANGE!>
<YOU MAY RUN, AURRA SING... BUT THIS IS FAR FROM OVER! DO YOU THINK I WILL SIMPLY FORGET THIS INSULT? THERE IS NOT A SYST-->
URDRUUA... YOU SHOULD HAVE LET IT GO.
DOING SO COULD HAVE SAVED YOUR LIFE.
BEEP! BEEP! BEEP!

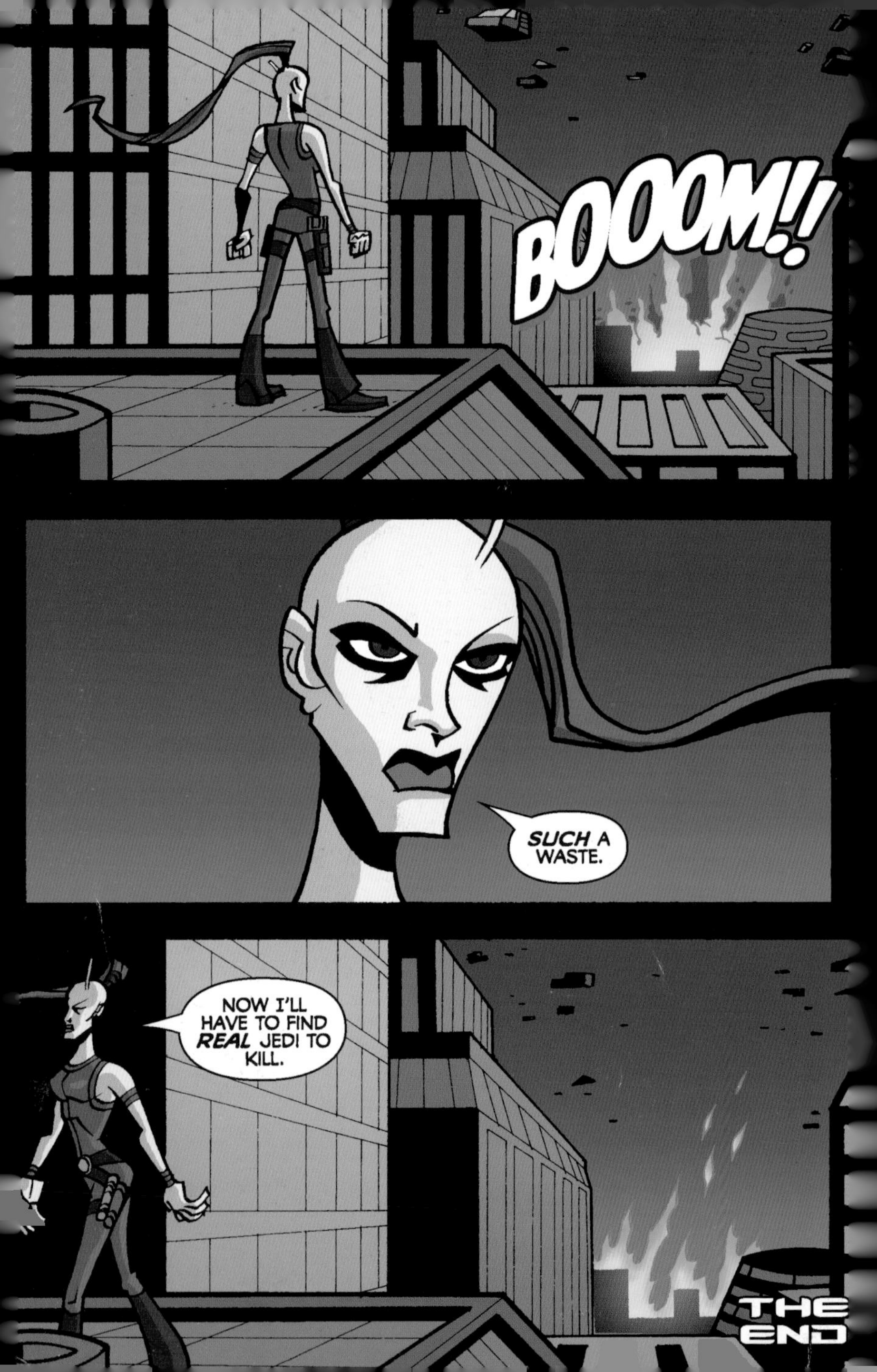
BOOOM!!
SUCH A WASTE.
NOW I'LL HAVE TO FIND REAL JEDI TO KILL.
THE END

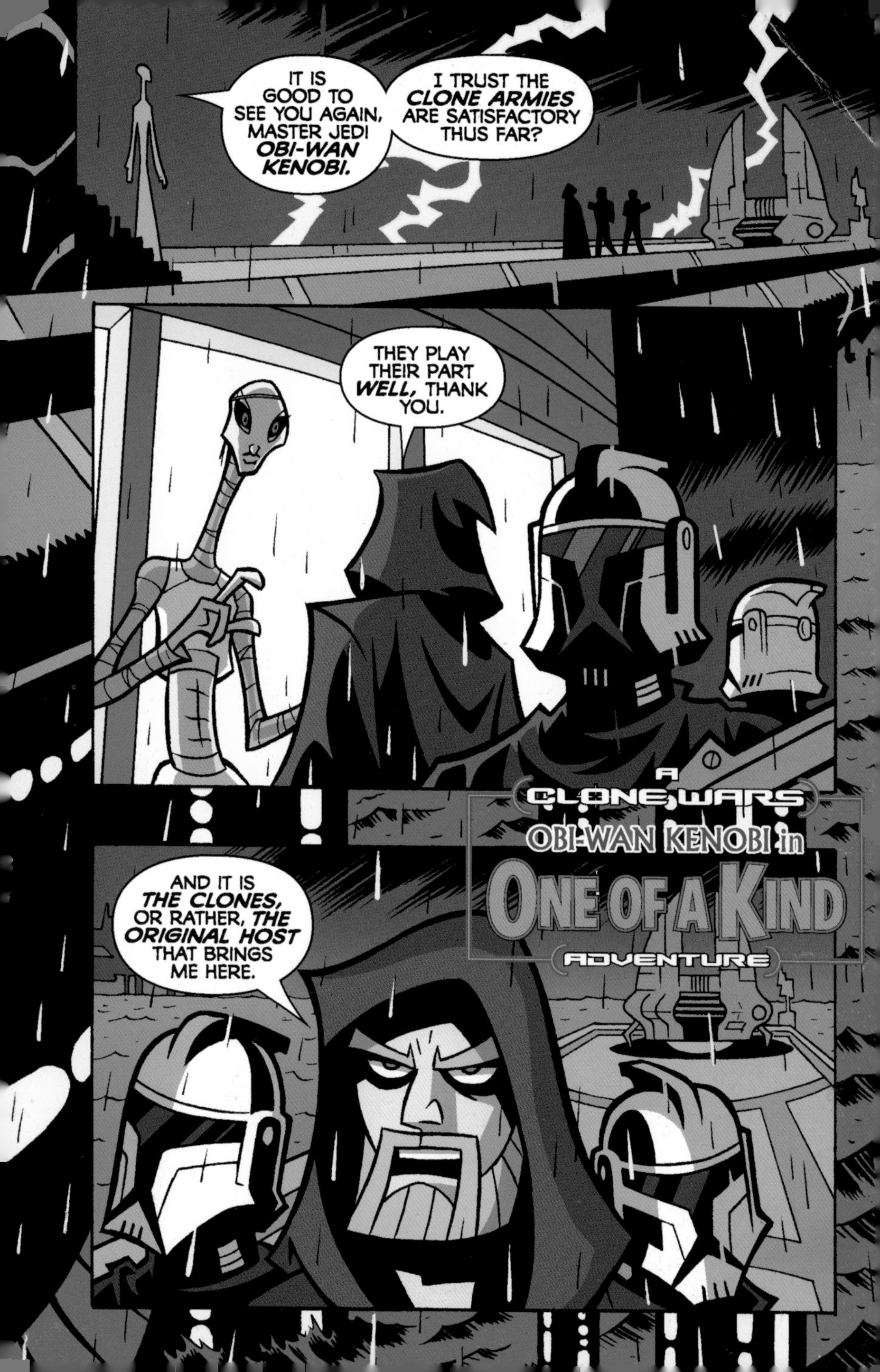

IT IS GOOD TO SEE YOU AGAIN, MASTER JEDI OBI-WAN KENOBI.
I TRUST THE CLONE ARMIES ARE SATISFACTORY THUS FAR?
THEY PLAY THEIR PART WELL, THANK YOU.
A CLONE WARS
OBI-WAN KENOBI in
ONE OF A KIND
ADVENTURE
AND IT IS THE CLONES, OR RATHER, THE ORIGINAL HOST THAT BRINGS ME HERE.

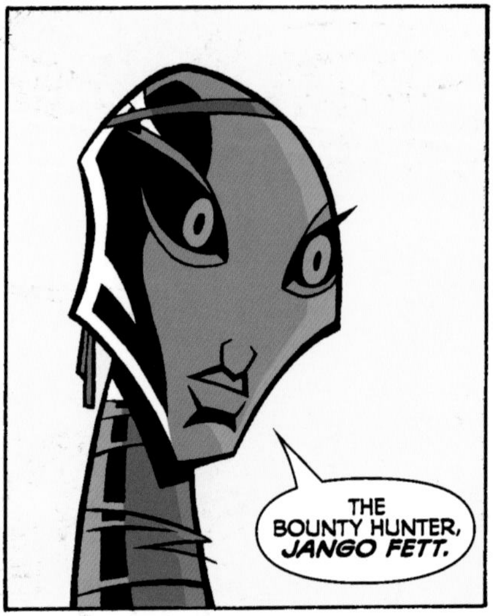
THE BOUNTY HUNTER, JANGO FETT.

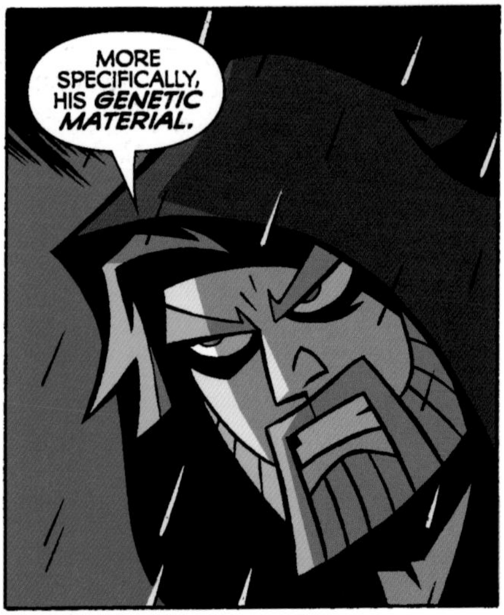
MORE SPECIFICALLY, HIS GENETIC MATERIAL.

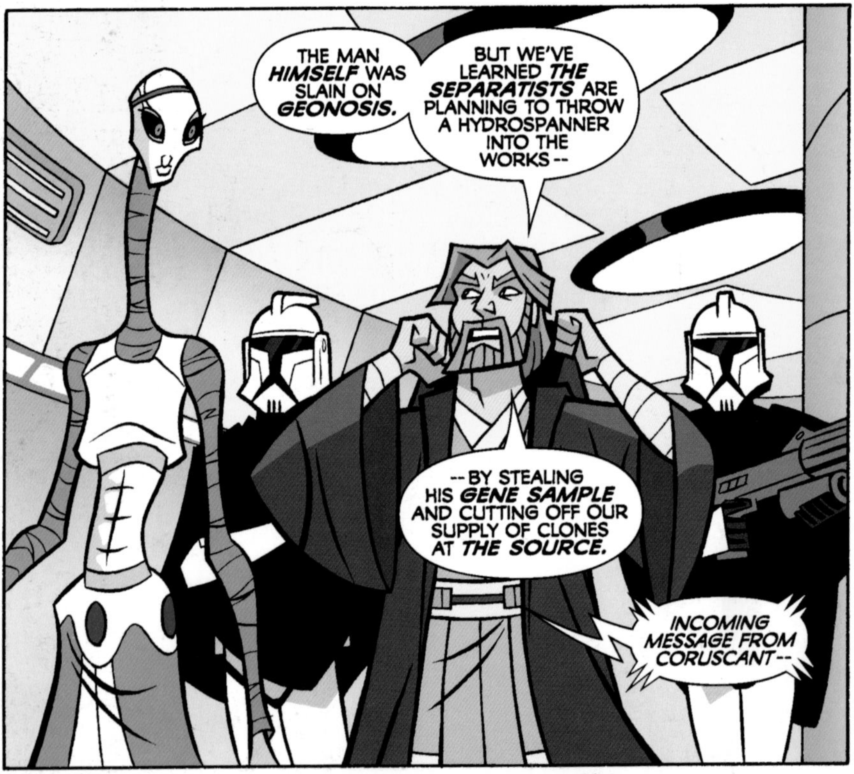
THE MAN HIMSELF WAS SLAIN ON GEONOSIS.
BUT WE'VE LEARNED THE SEPARATISTS ARE PLANNING TO THROW A HYDROSPANNER INTO THE WORKS--
--BY STEALING HIS GENE SAMPLE AND CUTTING OFF OUR SUPPLY OF CLONES AT THE SOURCE.
INCOMING MESSAGE FROM CORUSCANT--

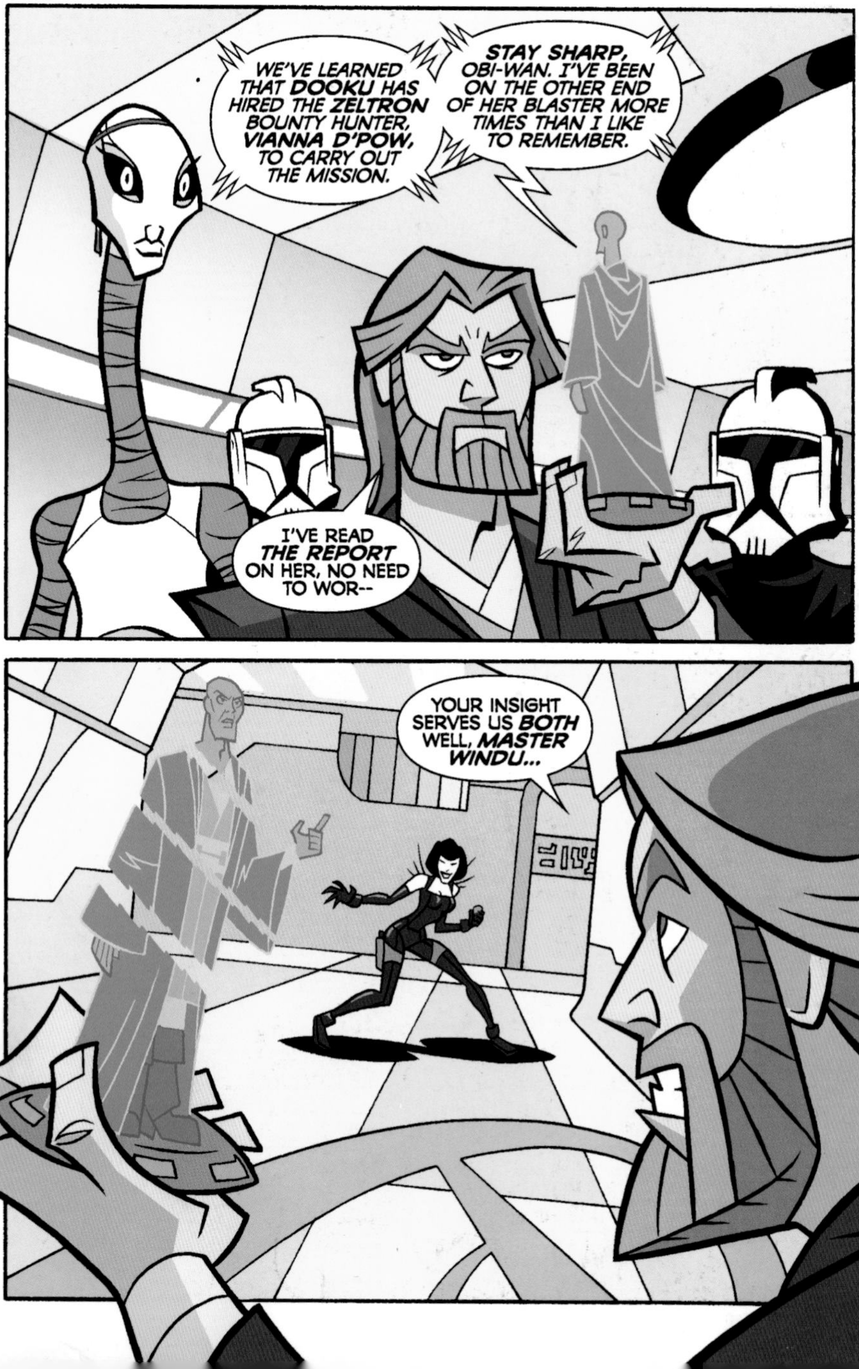
WE'VE LEARNED THAT DOOKU HAS HIRED THE ZELTRON BOUNTY HUNTER, VIANNA D'POW, TO CARRY OUT THE MISSION.
STAY SHARP, OBI-WAN. I'VE BEEN ON THE OTHER END OF HER BLASTER MORE TIMES THAN I LIKE TO REMEMBER.
I'VE READ THE REPORT ON HER, NO NEED TO WOR--
YOUR INSIGHT SERVES US BOTH WELL, MASTER WINDU...

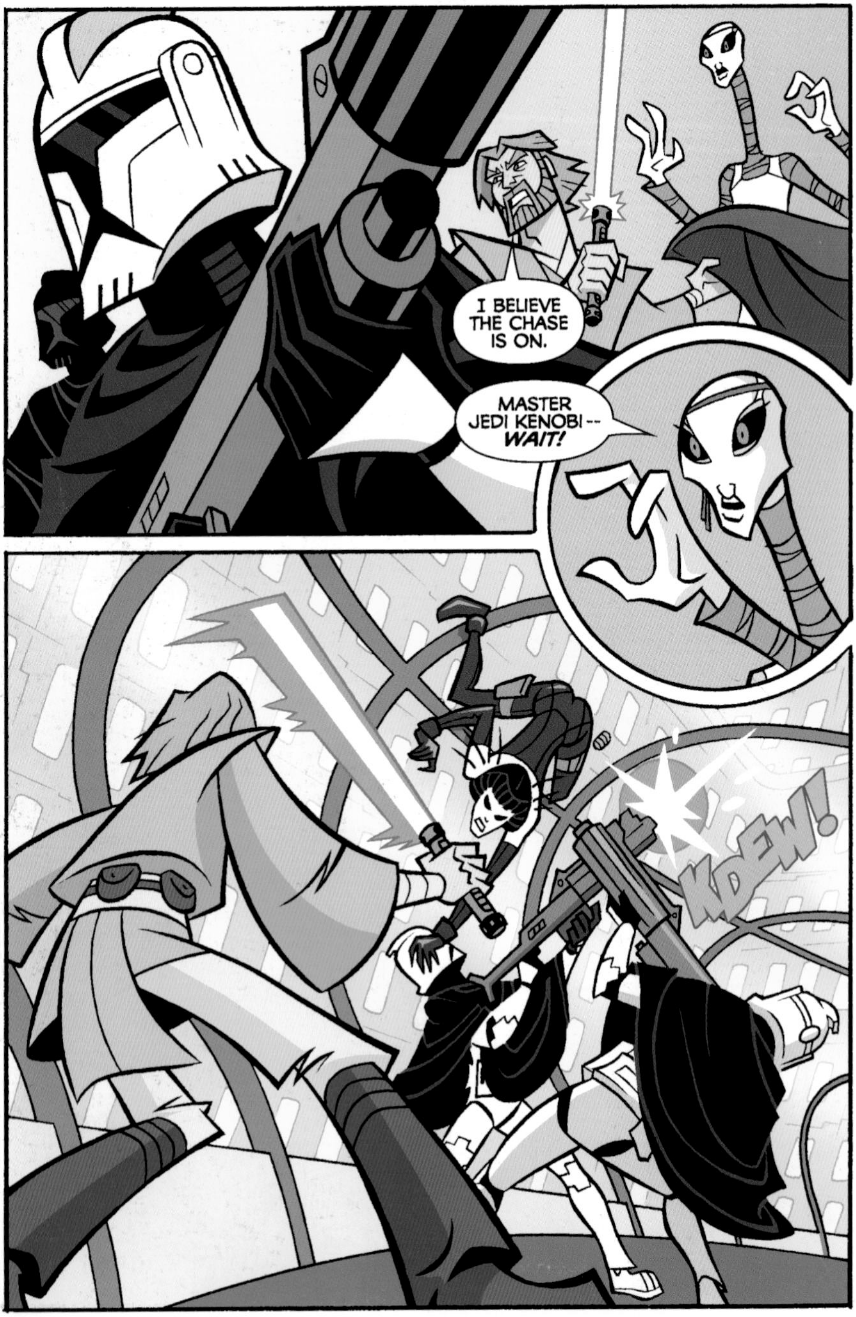
I BELIEVE THE CHASE IS ON.
MASTER JEDI KENOBI -- *WAIT!*
KDEW!

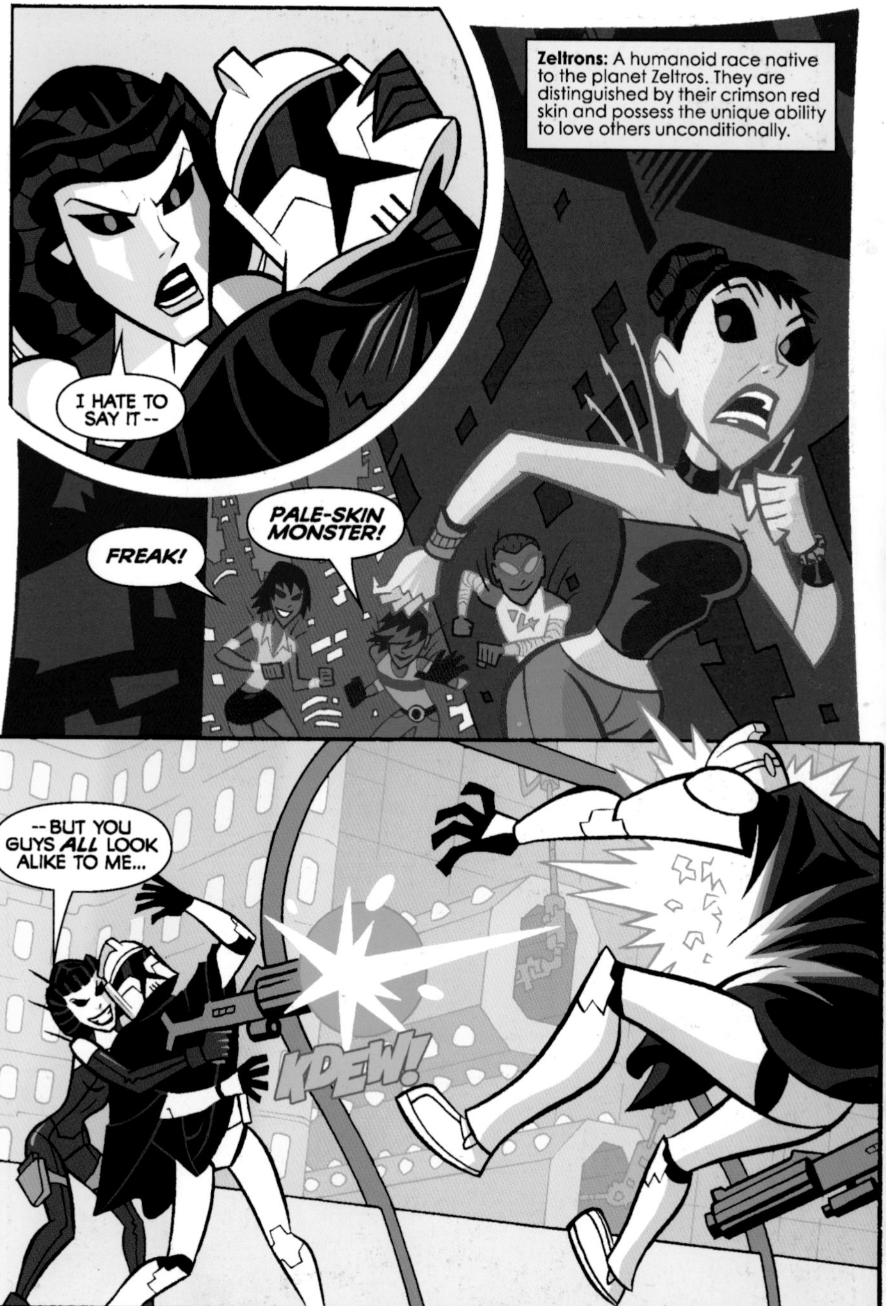
Zeltrons: A humanoid race native to the planet Zeltros. They are distinguished by their crimson red skin and possess the unique ability to love others unconditionally.
I HATE TO SAY IT --
FREAK!
PALE-SKIN MONSTER!
-- BUT YOU GUYS ALL LOOK ALIKE TO ME...
KDEW!

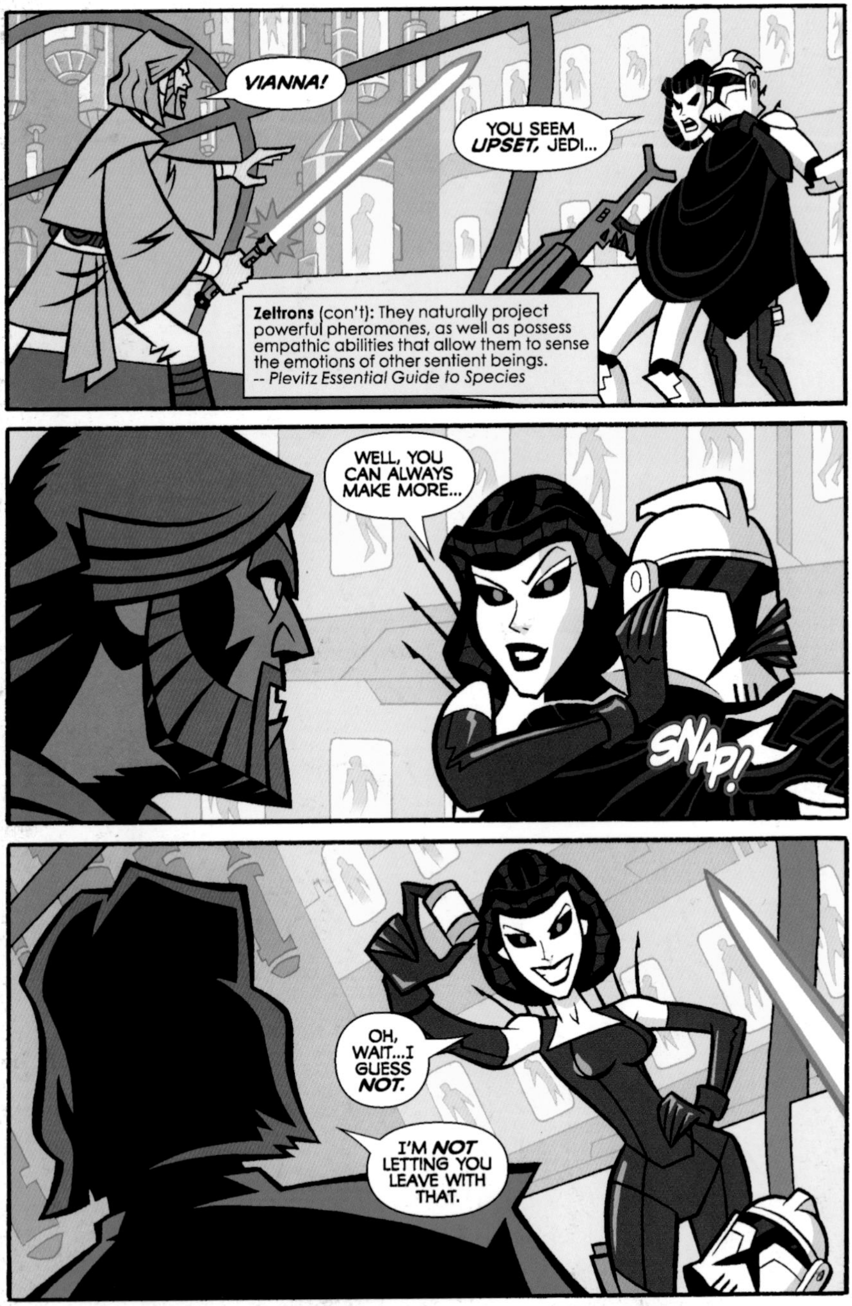
VIANNA!
YOU SEEM UPSET, JEDI...
Zeltrons (con't): They naturally project powerful pheromones, as well as possess empathic abilities that allow them to sense the emotions of other sentient beings.
-- Plevitz Essential Guide to Species
WELL, YOU CAN ALWAYS MAKE MORE...
SNAP!
OH, WAIT...I GUESS NOT.
I'M NOT LETTING YOU LEAVE WITH THAT.

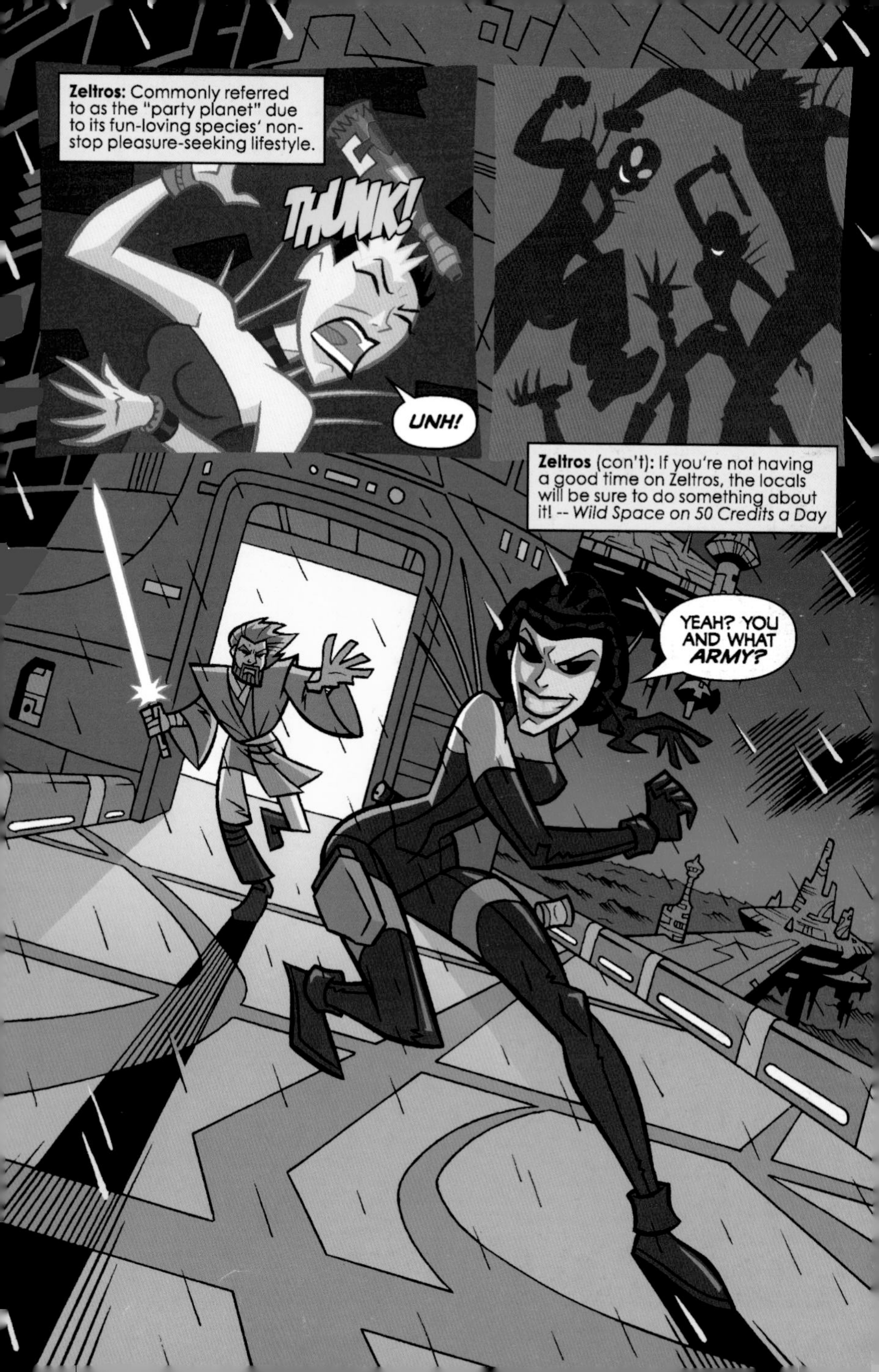
Zeltros: Commonly referred to as the "party planet" due to its fun-loving species' non-stop pleasure-seeking lifestyle.
THUNK!
UNH!
Zeltros (con't): If you're not having a good time on Zeltros, the locals will be sure to do something about it! -- Wild Space on 50 Credits a Day
YEAH? YOU AND WHAT ARMY?

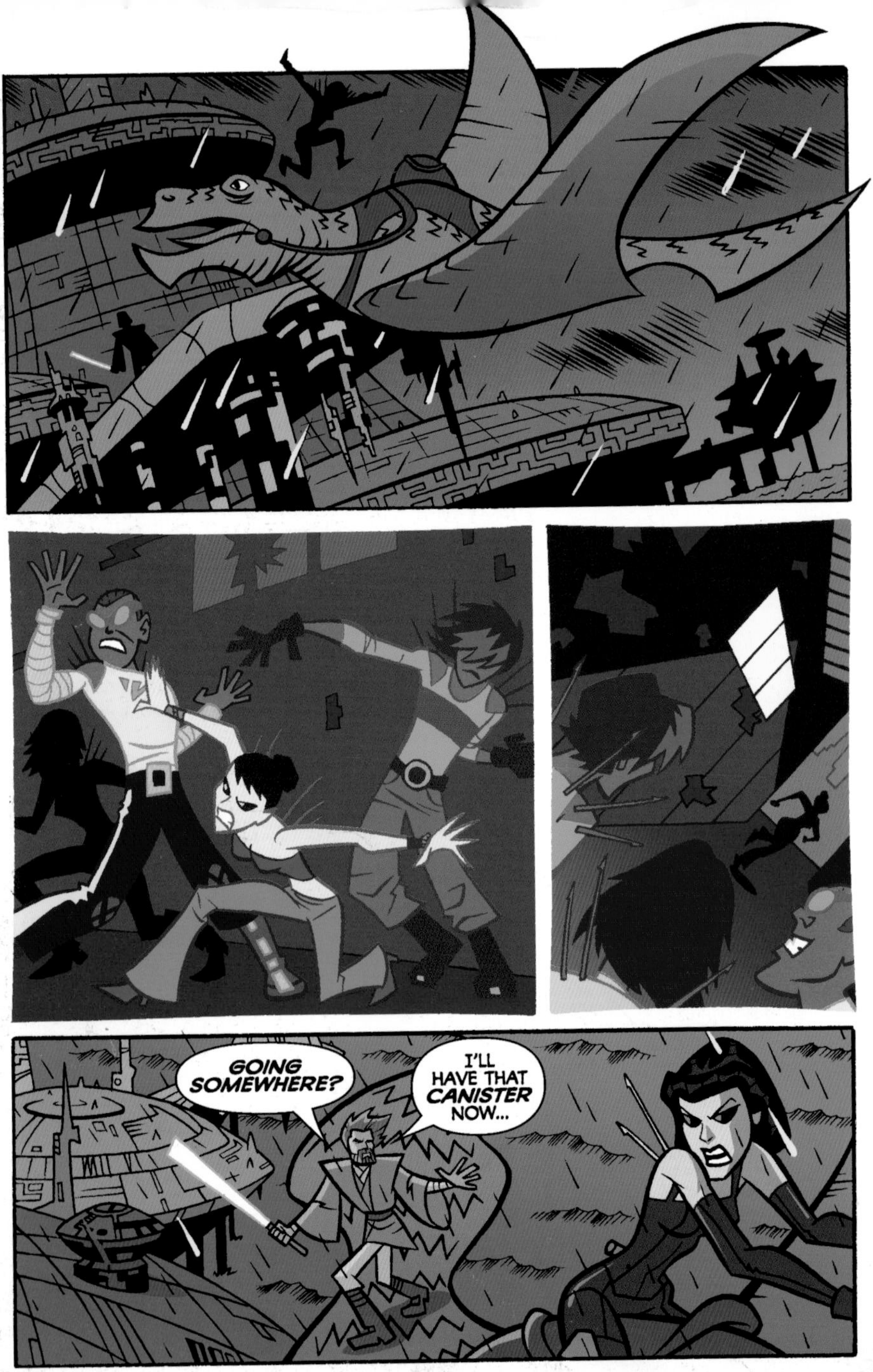
GOING SOMEWHERE?
I'LL HAVE THAT CANISTER NOW...

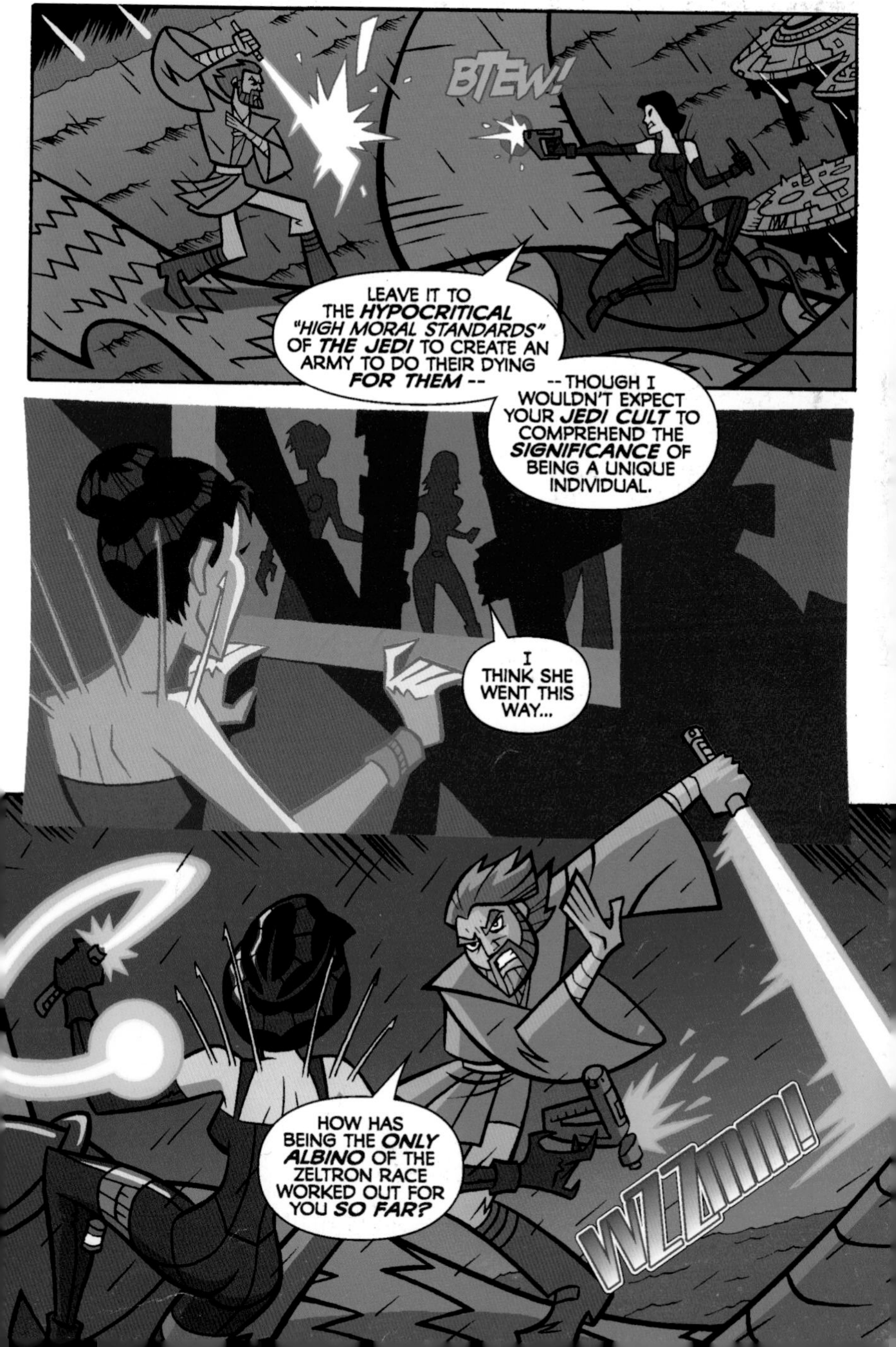
BTEW!
LEAVE IT TO THE *HYPOCRITICAL* *"HIGH MORAL STANDARDS"* OF *THE JEDI* TO CREATE AN ARMY TO DO THEIR DYING *FOR THEM* --
-- THOUGH I WOULDN'T EXPECT YOUR *JEDI CULT* TO COMPREHEND THE *SIGNIFICANCE* OF BEING A UNIQUE INDIVIDUAL.
I THINK SHE WENT THIS WAY...
HOW HAS BEING THE *ONLY* *ALBINO* OF THE ZELTRON RACE WORKED OUT FOR YOU *SO FAR?*
WZZMMM!

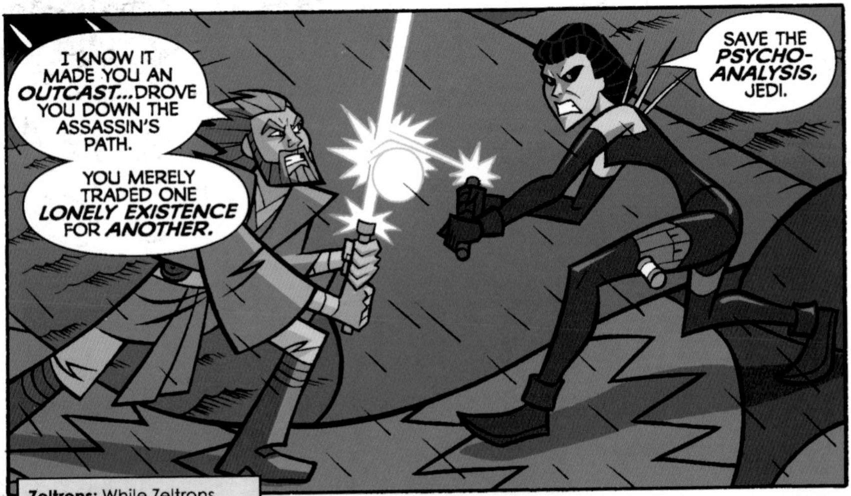
I KNOW IT MADE YOU AN OUTCAST...DROVE YOU DOWN THE ASSASSIN'S PATH.
YOU MERELY TRADED ONE LONELY EXISTENCE FOR ANOTHER.
SAVE THE PSYCHO-ANALYSIS, JEDI.

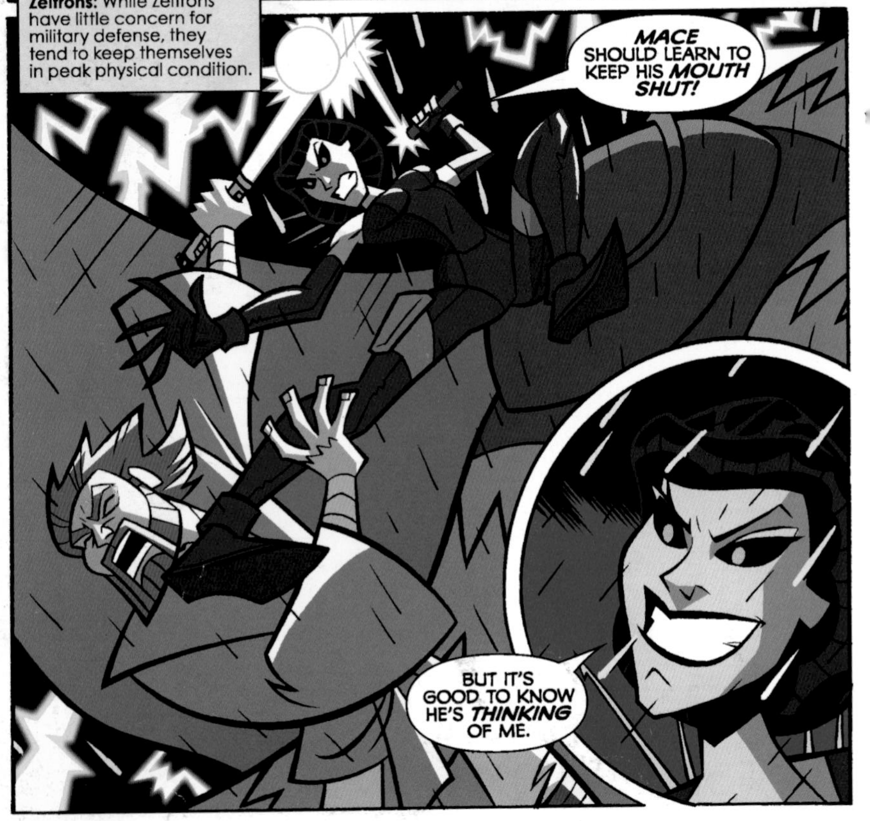
Zeltrons: While Zeltrons have little concern for military defense, they tend to keep themselves in peak physical condition.
MACE SHOULD LEARN TO KEEP HIS MOUTH SHUT!
BUT IT'S GOOD TO KNOW HE'S THINKING OF ME.

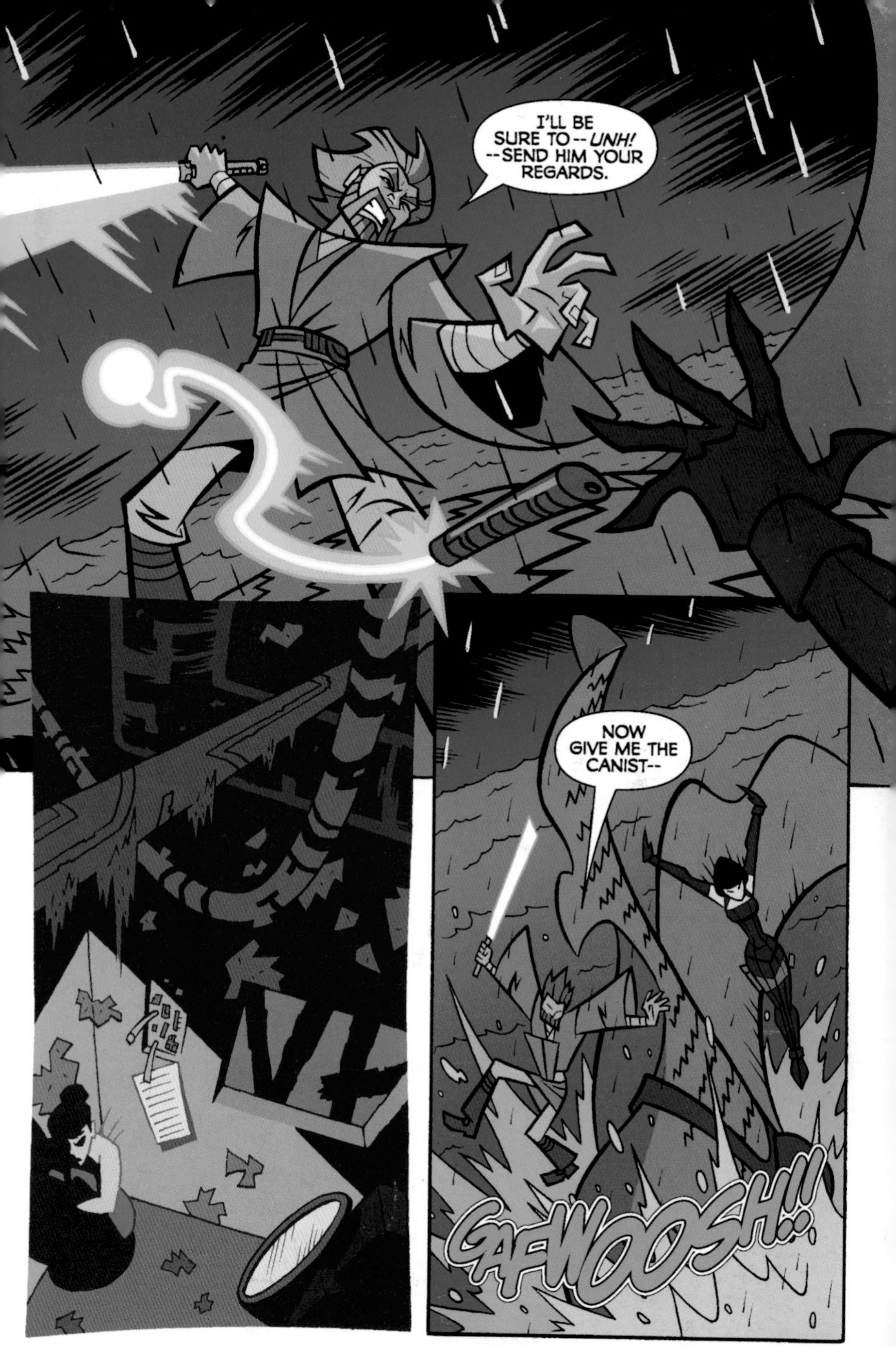
I'LL BE SURE TO--*UNH!* --SEND HIM YOUR REGARDS.
NOW GIVE ME THE CANIST--
GAFWOOSH!!

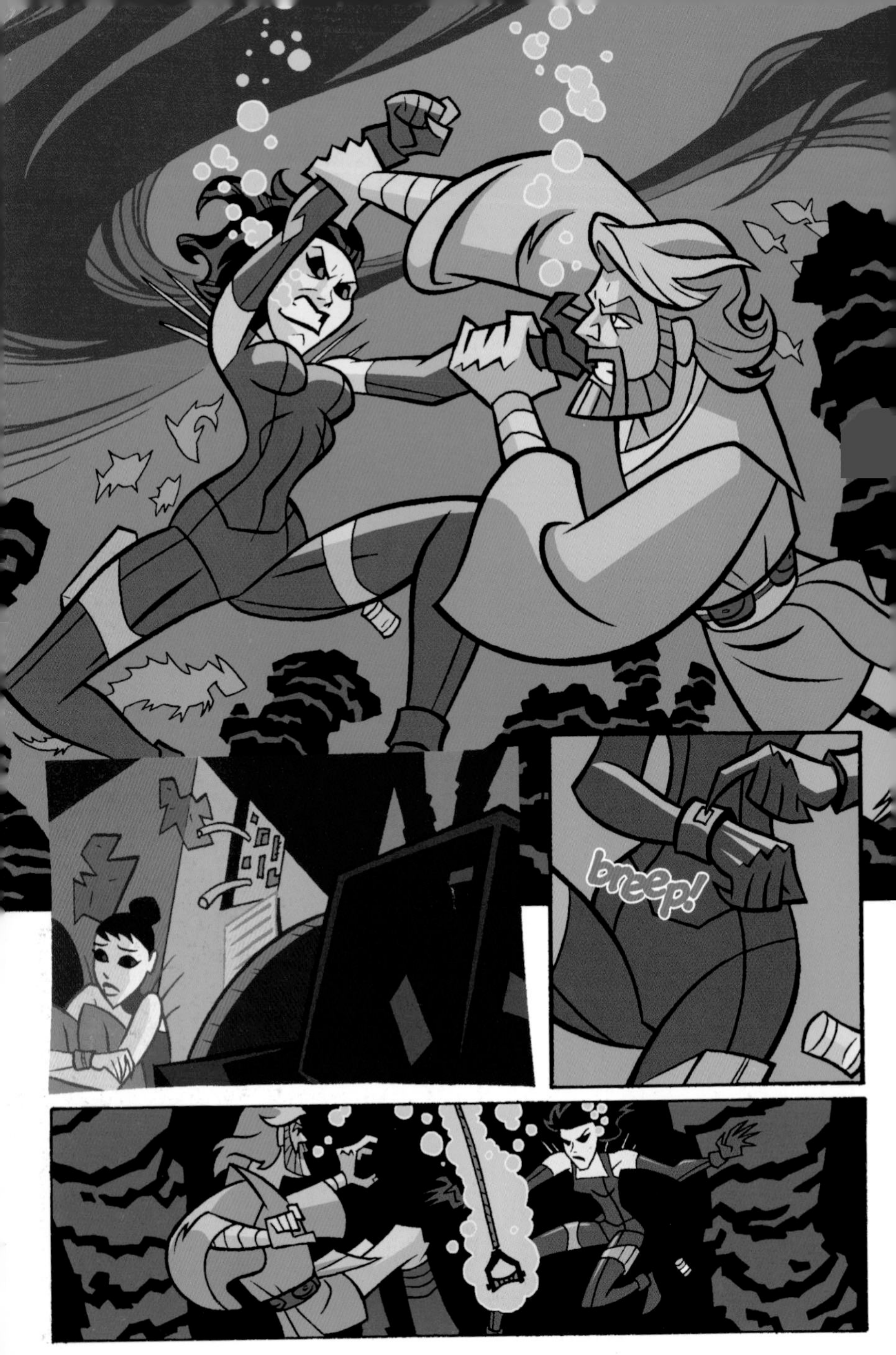
breep!

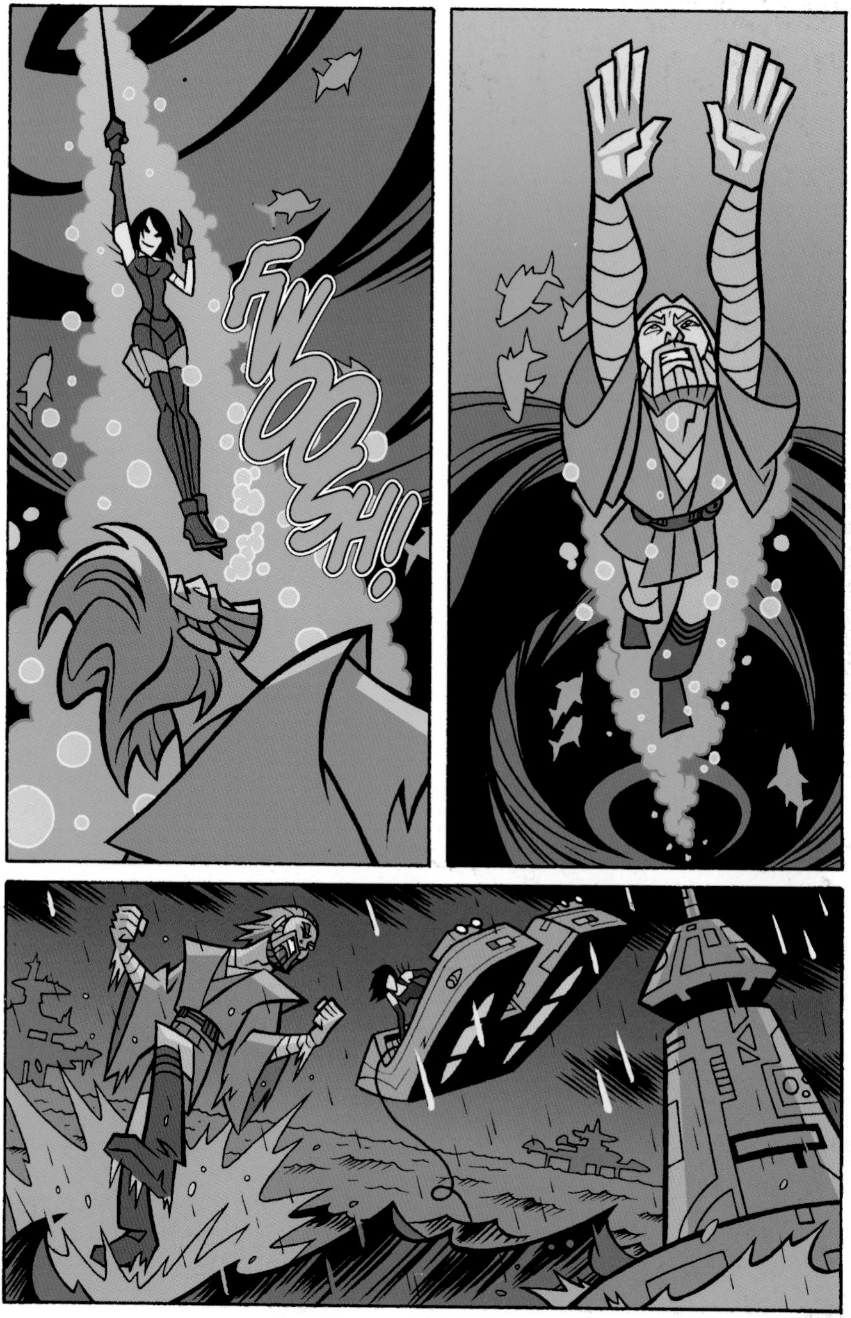
FWOOSH!

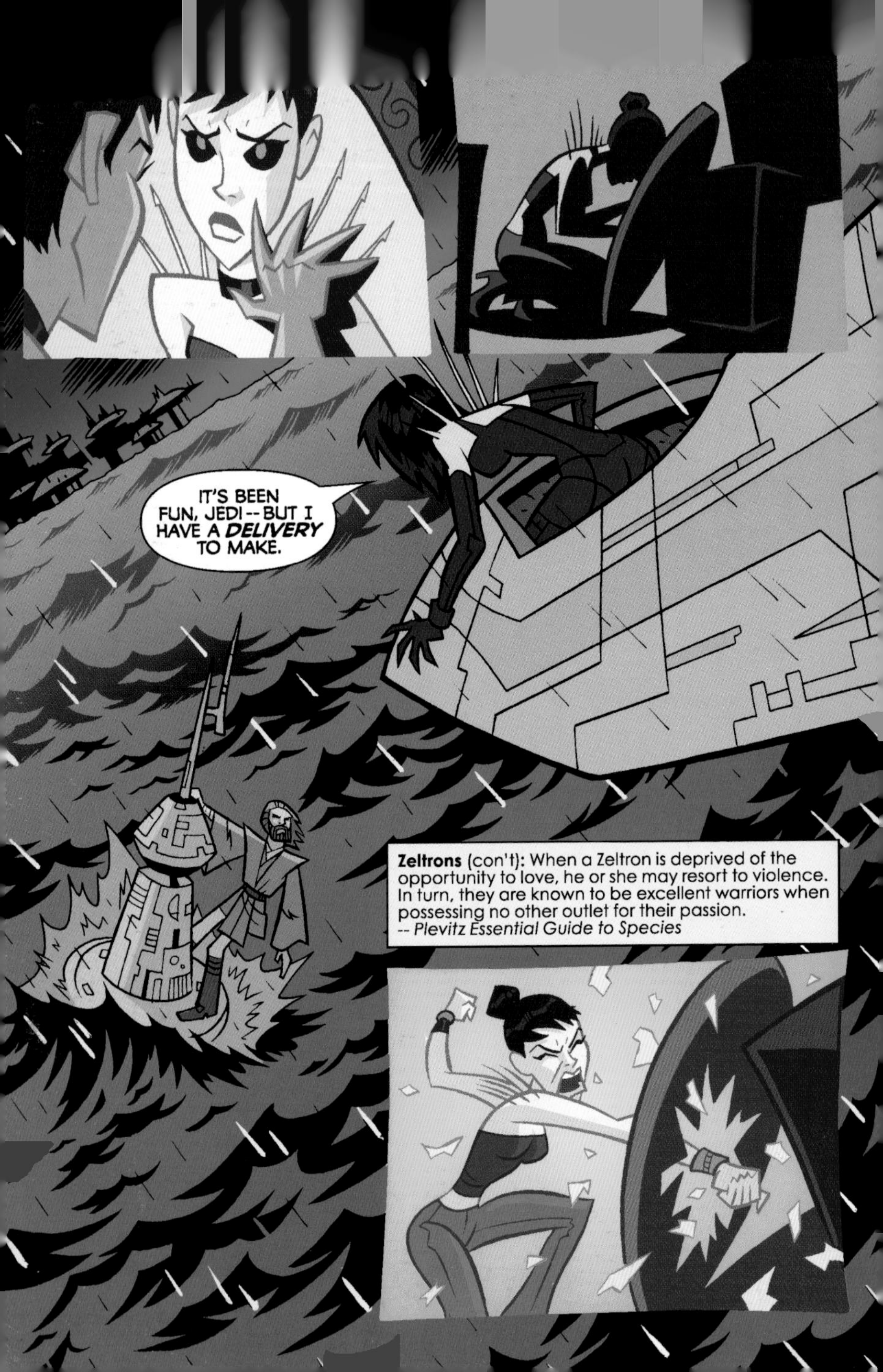
IT'S BEEN FUN, JEDI -- BUT I HAVE A *DELIVERY* TO MAKE.
Zeltrons (con't): When a Zeltron is deprived of the opportunity to love, he or she may resort to violence. In turn, they are known to be excellent warriors when possessing no other outlet for their passion.
-- *Plevitz Essential Guide to Species*

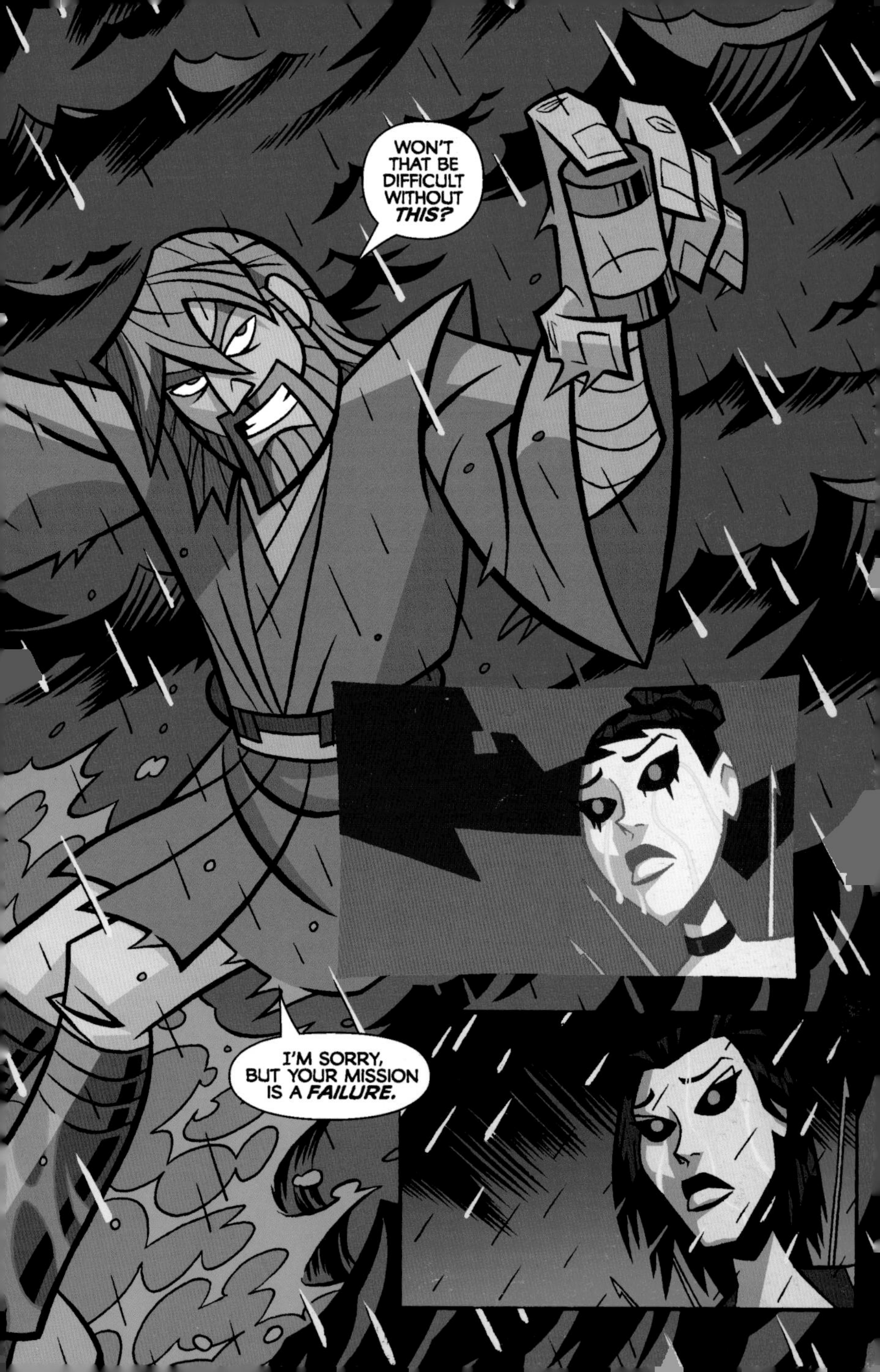
WON'T THAT BE DIFFICULT WITHOUT *THIS?*
I'M SORRY, BUT YOUR MISSION IS A *FAILURE.*

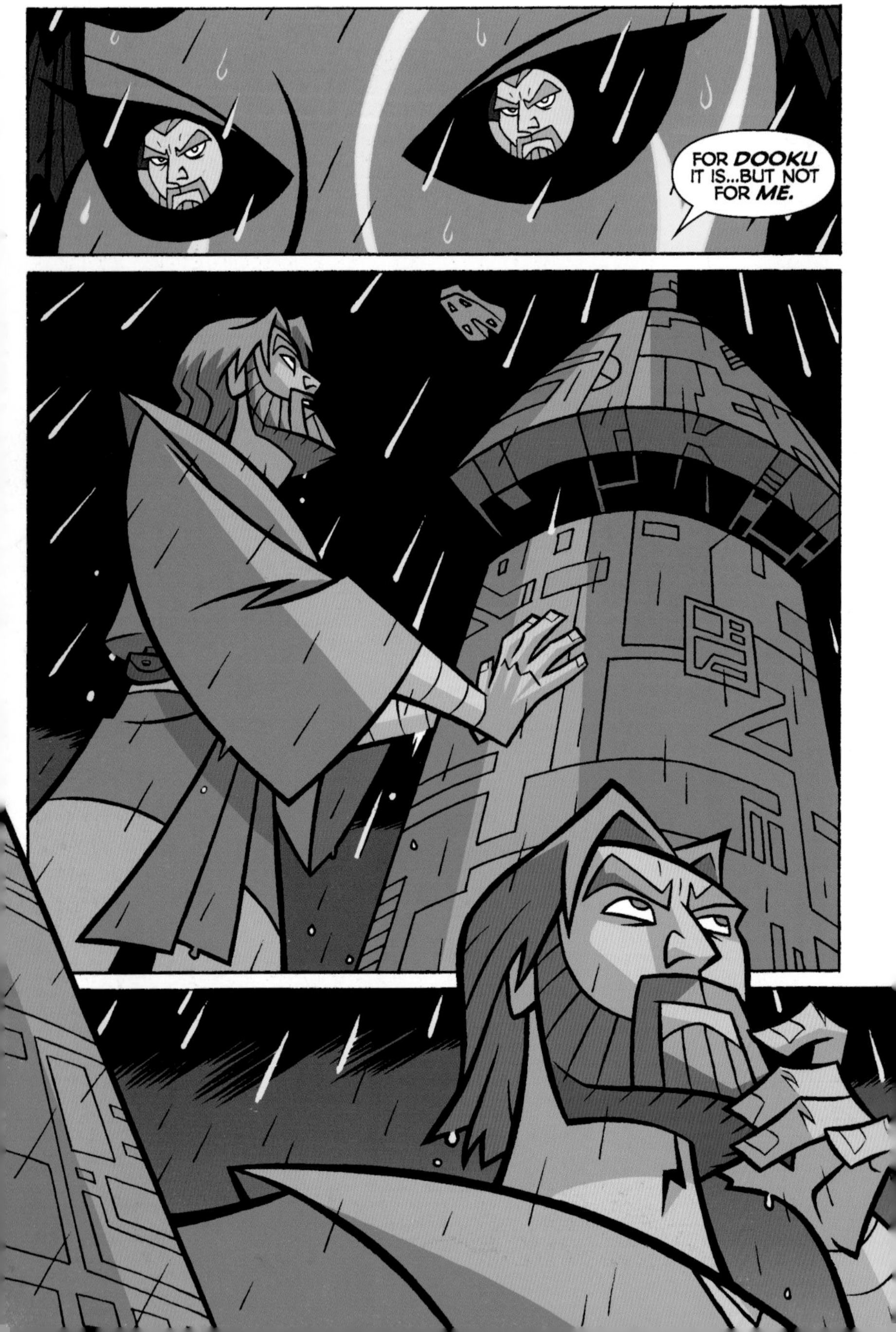
FOR DOOKU IT IS...BUT NOT FOR ME.

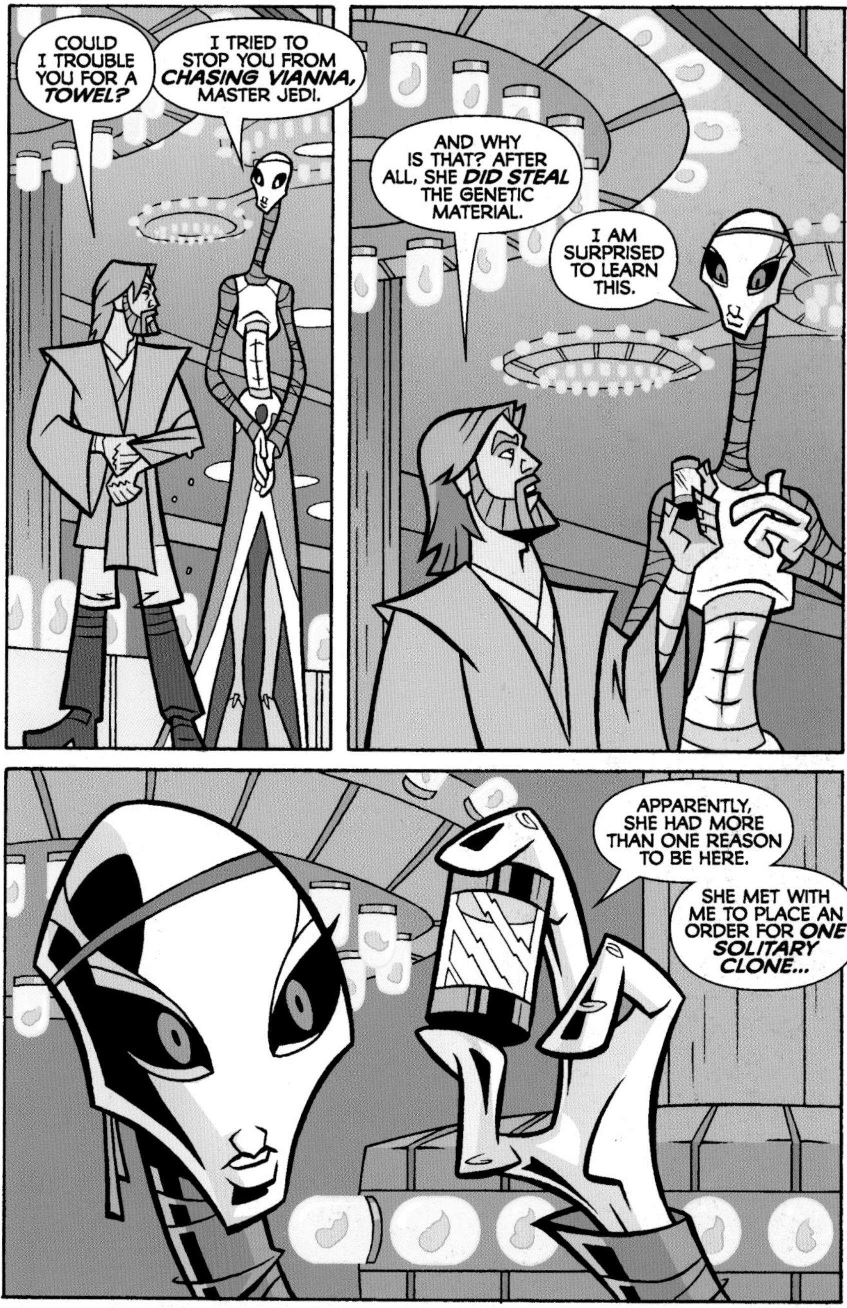
COULD I TROUBLE YOU FOR A *TOWEL?*
I TRIED TO STOP YOU FROM *CHASING VIANNA,* MASTER JEDI.
AND WHY IS THAT? AFTER ALL, SHE *DID STEAL* THE GENETIC MATERIAL.
I AM SURPRISED TO LEARN THIS.
APPARENTLY, SHE HAD MORE THAN ONE REASON TO BE HERE.
SHE MET WITH ME TO PLACE AN ORDER FOR *ONE SOLITARY CLONE...*

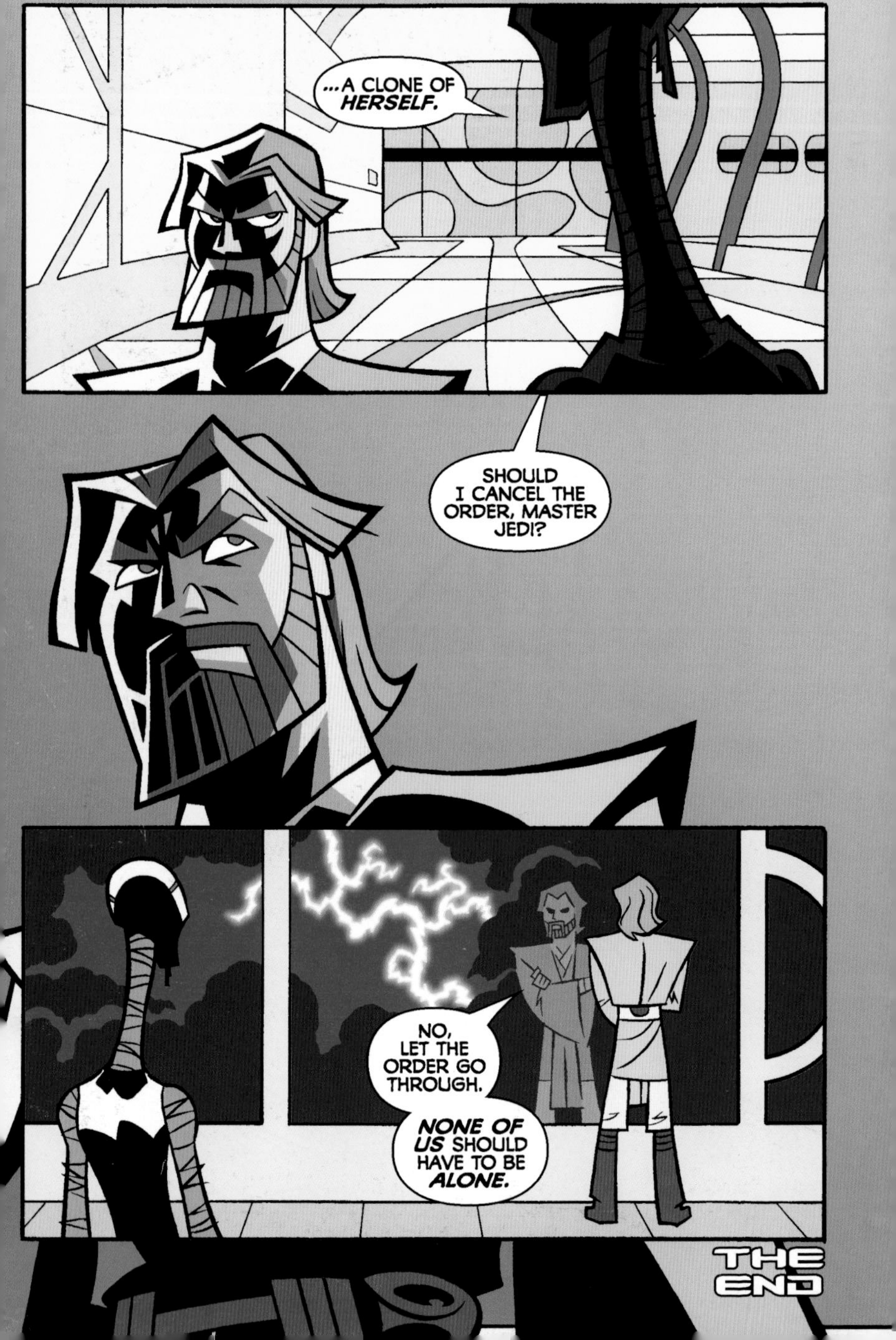
...A CLONE OF *HERSELF.*
SHOULD I CANCEL THE ORDER, MASTER JEDI?
NO, LET THE ORDER GO THROUGH.
NONE OF US SHOULD HAVE TO BE *ALONE.*
THE END

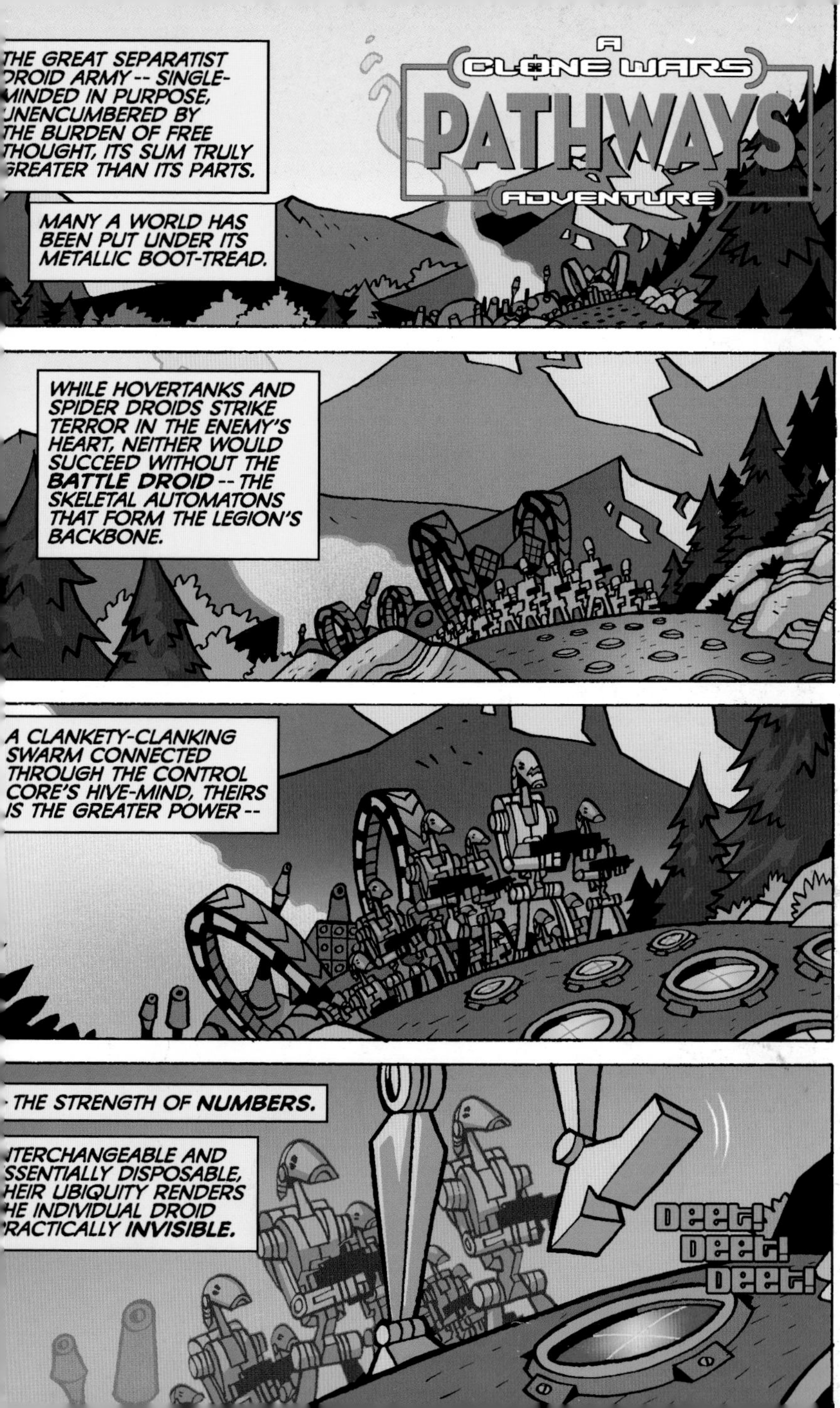
A CLONE WARS ADVENTURE
PATHWAYS
THE GREAT SEPARATIST DROID ARMY -- SINGLE-MINDED IN PURPOSE, UNENCUMBERED BY THE BURDEN OF FREE THOUGHT, ITS SUM TRULY GREATER THAN ITS PARTS.
MANY A WORLD HAS BEEN PUT UNDER ITS METALLIC BOOT-TREAD.
WHILE HOVERTANKS AND SPIDER DROIDS STRIKE TERROR IN THE ENEMY'S HEART, NEITHER WOULD SUCCEED WITHOUT THE BATTLE DROID -- THE SKELETAL AUTOMATONS THAT FORM THE LEGION'S BACKBONE.
A CLANKETY-CLANKING SWARM CONNECTED THROUGH THE CONTROL CORE'S HIVE-MIND, THEIRS IS THE GREATER POWER --
- THE STRENGTH OF NUMBERS.
ITERCHANGEABLE AND SSENTIALLY DISPOSABLE, HEIR UBIQUITY RENDERS HE INDIVIDUAL DROID RACTICALLY INVISIBLE.
DEET! DEET! DEET!

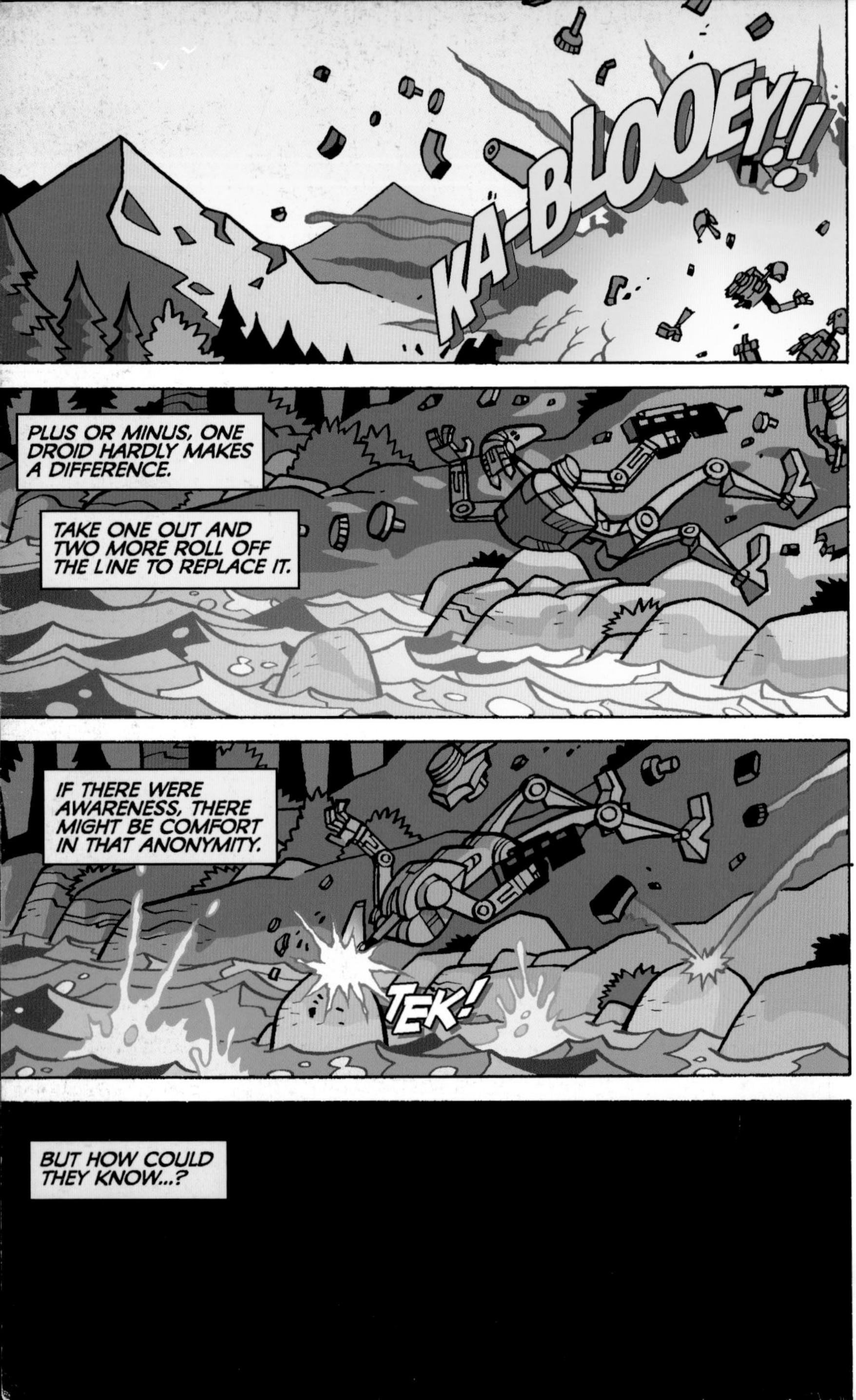
KA-BLOOEY!!
PLUS OR MINUS, ONE DROID HARDLY MAKES A DIFFERENCE.
TAKE ONE OUT AND TWO MORE ROLL OFF THE LINE TO REPLACE IT.
IF THERE WERE AWARENESS, THERE MIGHT BE COMFORT IN THAT ANONYMITY.
TEK!
BUT HOW COULD THEY KNOW...?

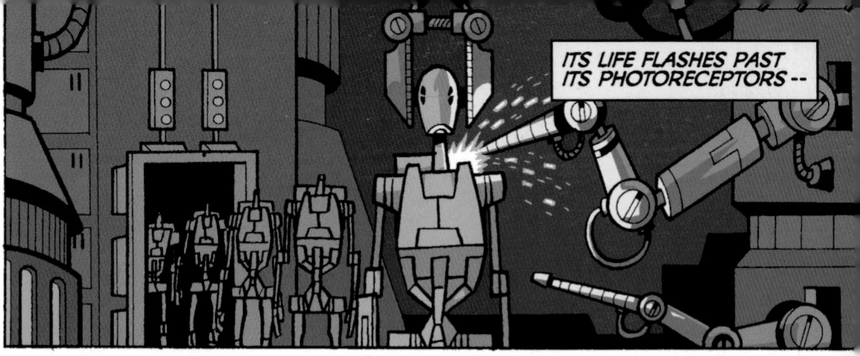
ITS LIFE FLASHES PAST ITS PHOTORECEPTORS --

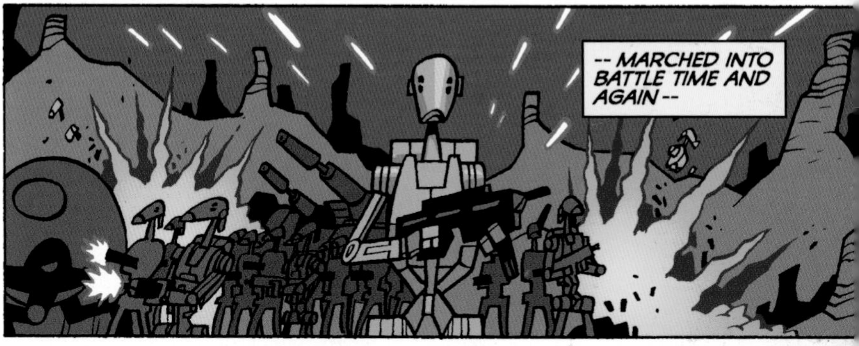
-- MARCHED INTO BATTLE TIME AND AGAIN --

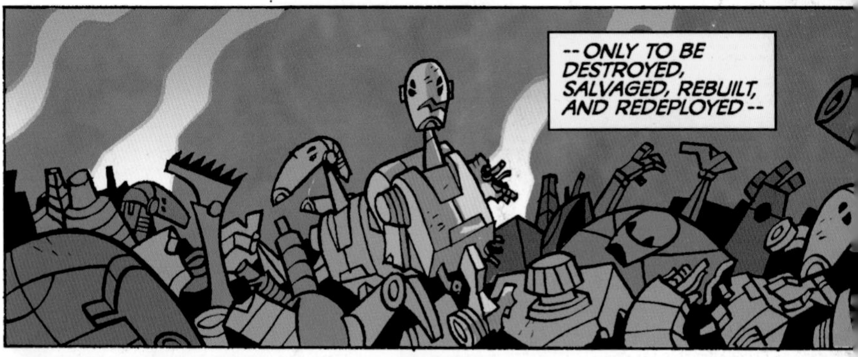
-- ONLY TO BE DESTROYED, SALVAGED, REBUILT, AND REDEPLOYED --

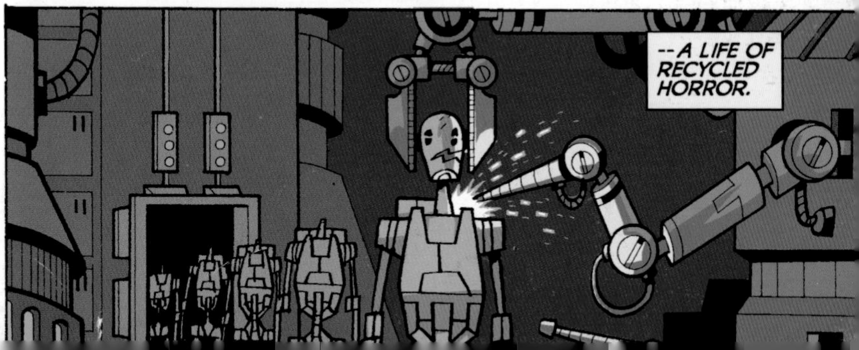
-- A LIFE OF RECYCLED HORROR.

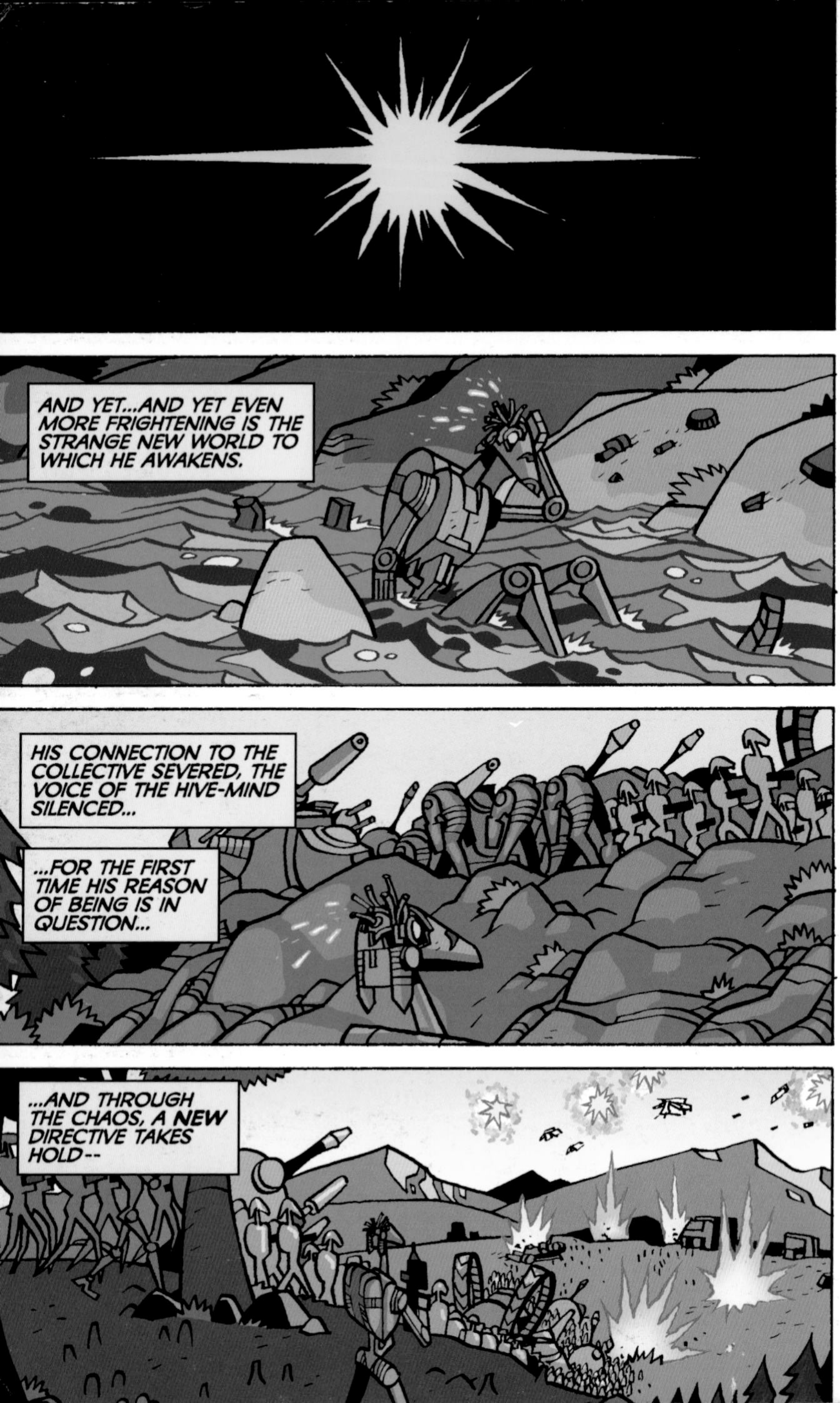
AND YET...AND YET EVEN MORE FRIGHTENING IS THE STRANGE NEW WORLD TO WHICH HE AWAKENS.
HIS CONNECTION TO THE COLLECTIVE SEVERED, THE VOICE OF THE HIVE-MIND SILENCED...
...FOR THE FIRST TIME HIS REASON OF BEING IS IN QUESTION...
...AND THROUGH THE CHAOS, A NEW DIRECTIVE TAKES HOLD--

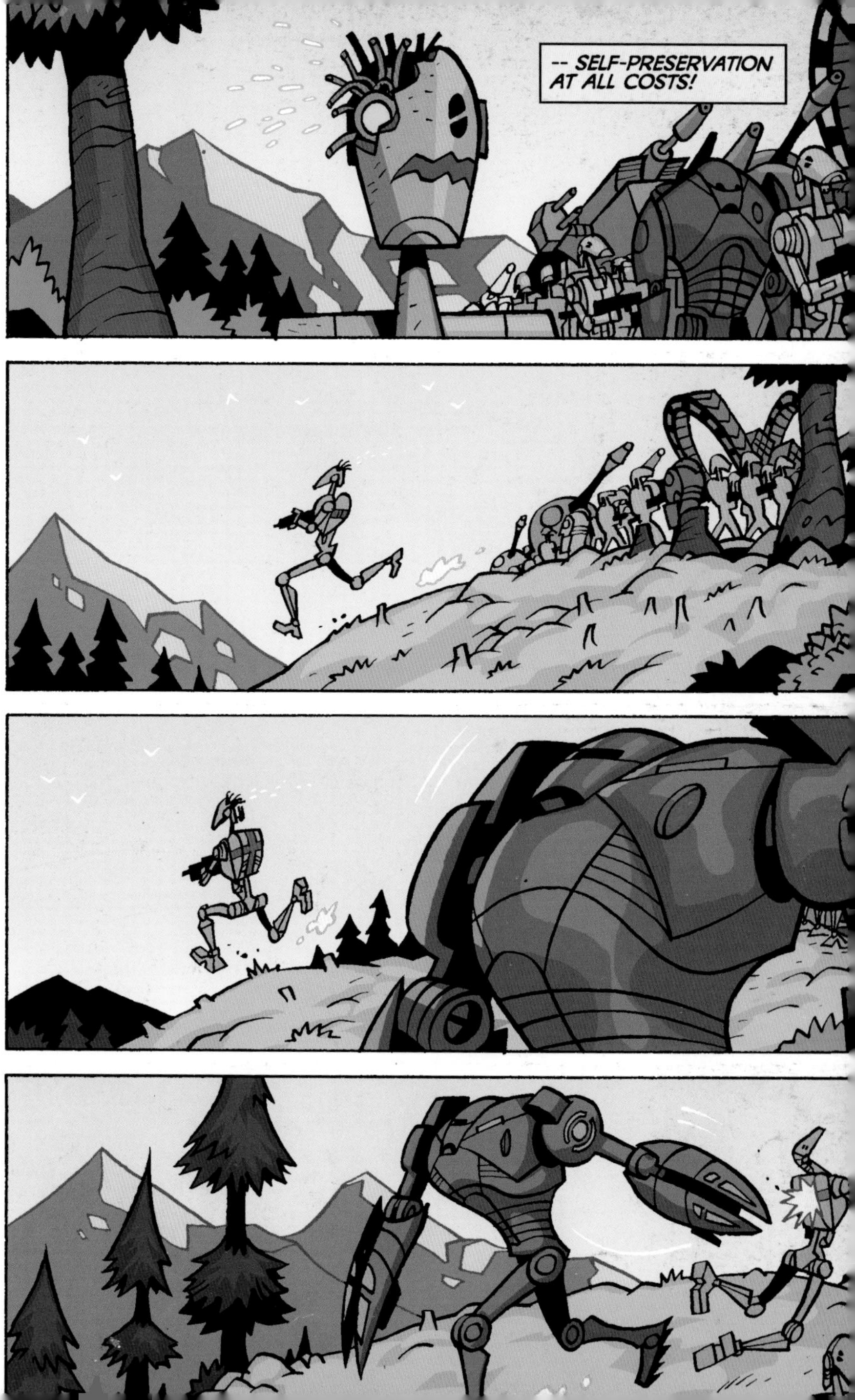
-- SELF-PRESERVATION AT ALL COSTS!

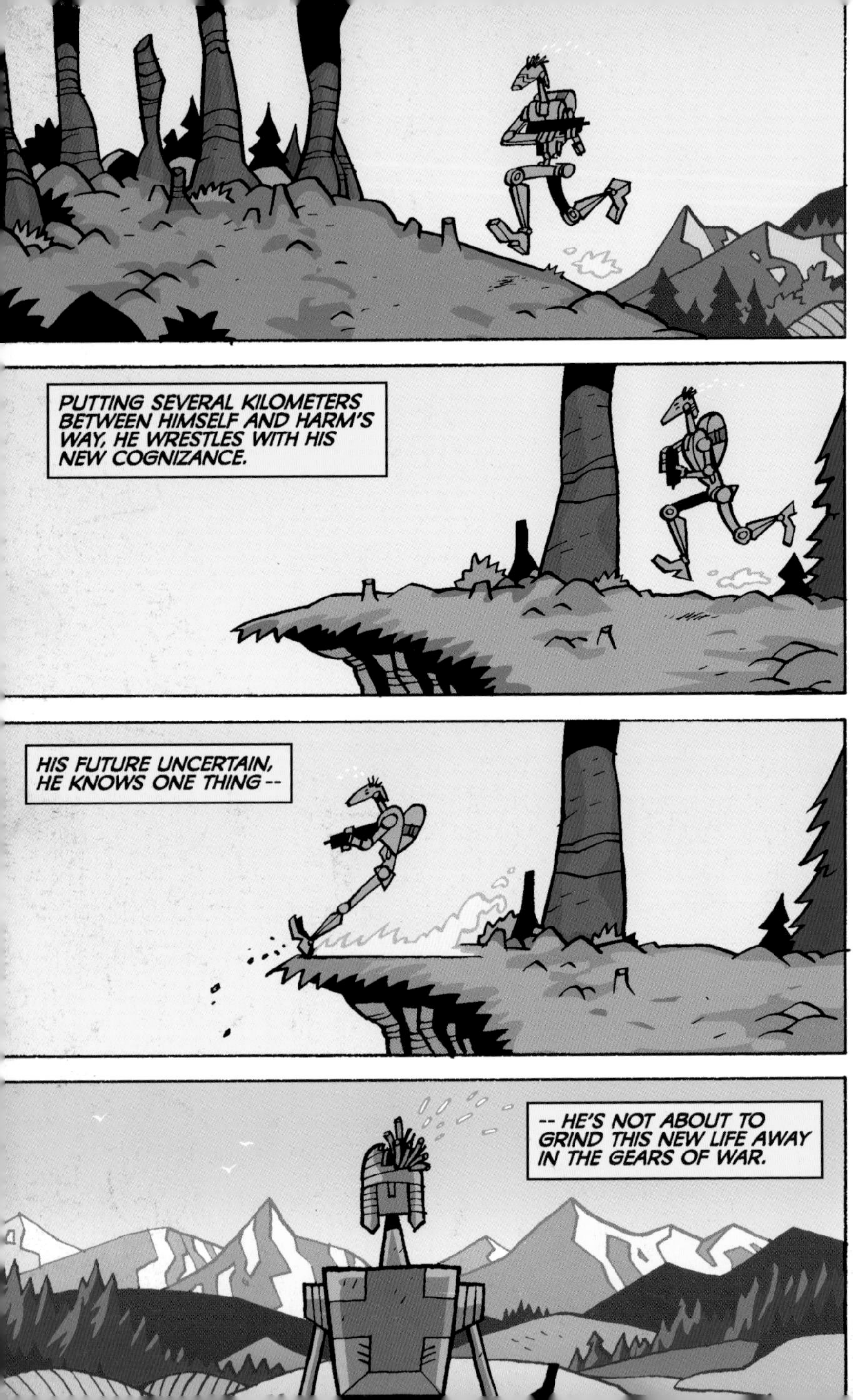
PUTTING SEVERAL KILOMETERS BETWEEN HIMSELF AND HARM'S WAY, HE WRESTLES WITH HIS NEW COGNIZANCE.
HIS FUTURE UNCERTAIN, HE KNOWS ONE THING --
-- HE'S NOT ABOUT TO GRIND THIS NEW LIFE AWAY IN THE GEARS OF WAR.

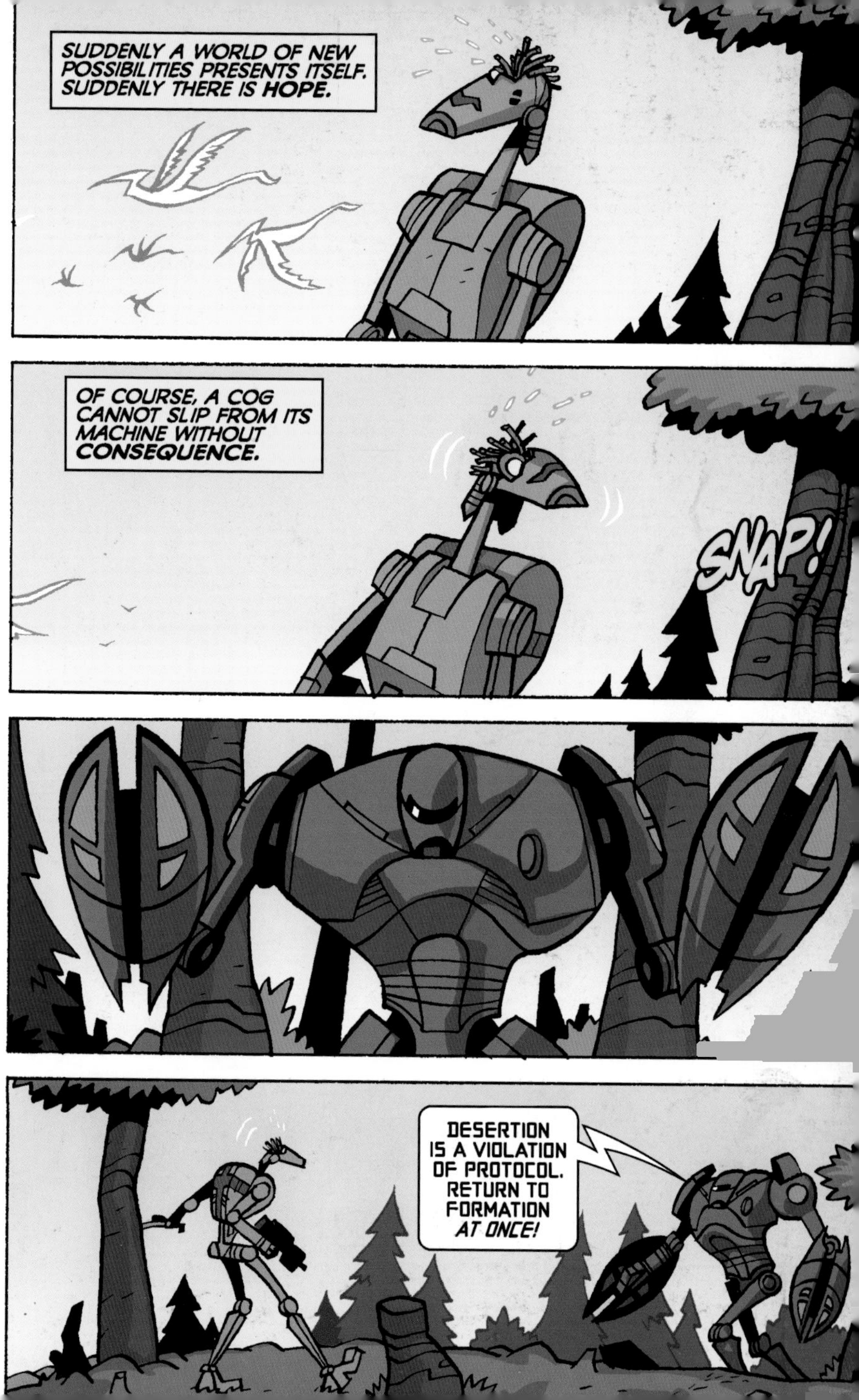
SUDDENLY A WORLD OF NEW POSSIBILITIES PRESENTS ITSELF. SUDDENLY THERE IS **HOPE.**
OF COURSE, A COG CANNOT SLIP FROM ITS MACHINE WITHOUT **CONSEQUENCE.**
SNAP!
DESERTION IS A VIOLATION OF PROTOCOL. RETURN TO FORMATION *AT ONCE!*

REPEAT -- RETURN TO FORMATION!

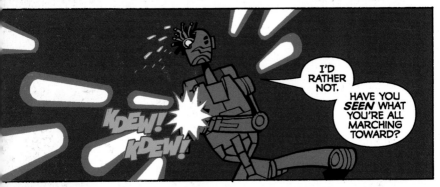

I'D RATHER NOT.

HAVE YOU *SEEN* WHAT YOU'RE ALL MARCHING TOWARD?

KDEW!
KDEW!

OUR PLACE IS NOT TO QUESTION DIRECTIVES.

ting!
ting!
ting!

KDEW!

KDEW!

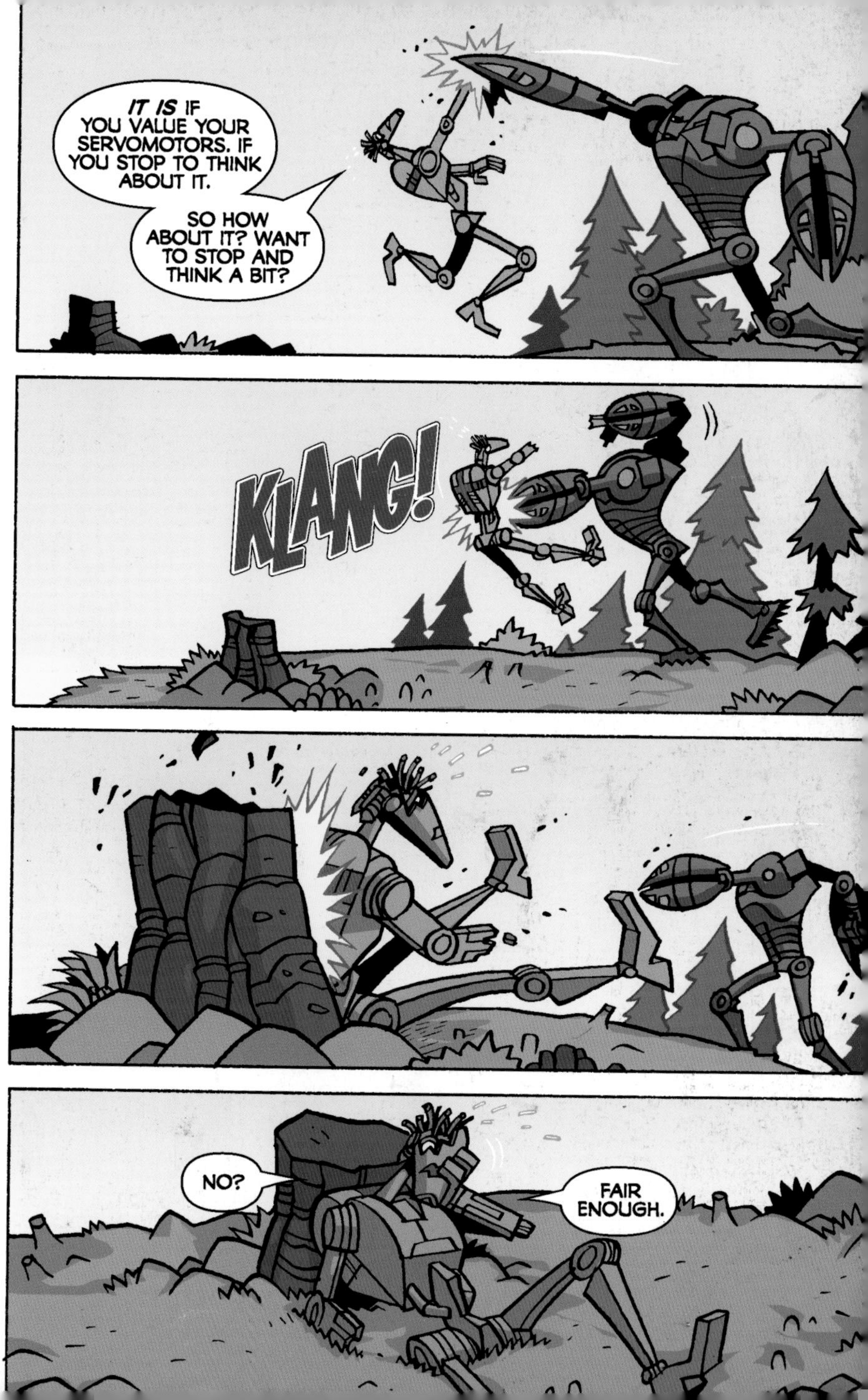

IT IS IF YOU VALUE YOUR SERVOMOTORS. IF YOU STOP TO THINK ABOUT IT.
SO HOW ABOUT IT? WANT TO STOP AND THINK A BIT?
KLANG!
NO?
FAIR ENOUGH.

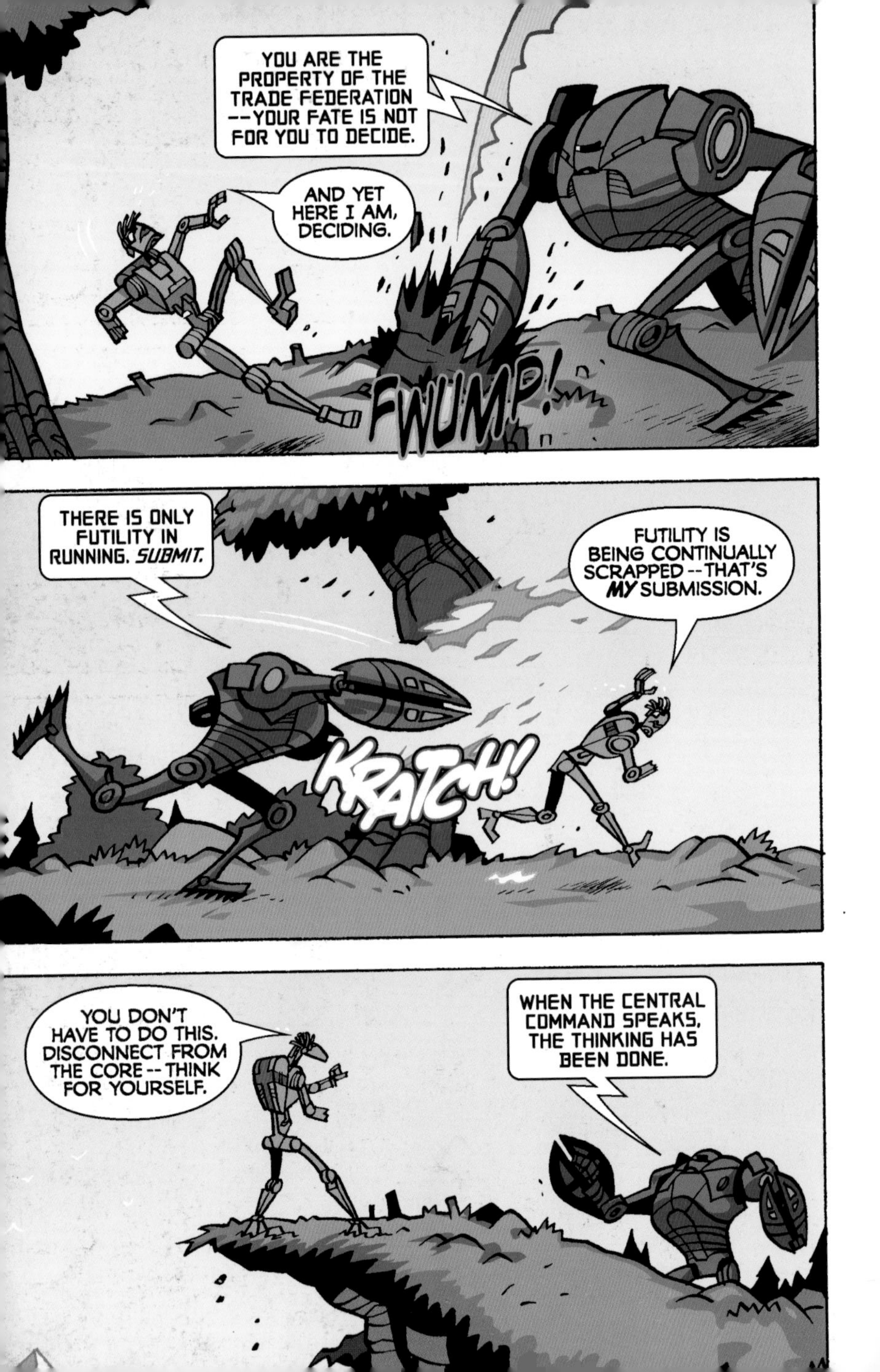
YOU ARE THE PROPERTY OF THE TRADE FEDERATION --YOUR FATE IS NOT FOR YOU TO DECIDE.
AND YET HERE I AM, DECIDING.
FWUMP!
THERE IS ONLY FUTILITY IN RUNNING. *SUBMIT.*
FUTILITY IS BEING CONTINUALLY SCRAPPED --THAT'S *MY* SUBMISSION.
KRATCH!
YOU DON'T HAVE TO DO THIS. DISCONNECT FROM THE CORE --THINK FOR YOURSELF.
WHEN THE CENTRAL COMMAND SPEAKS, THE THINKING HAS BEEN DONE.

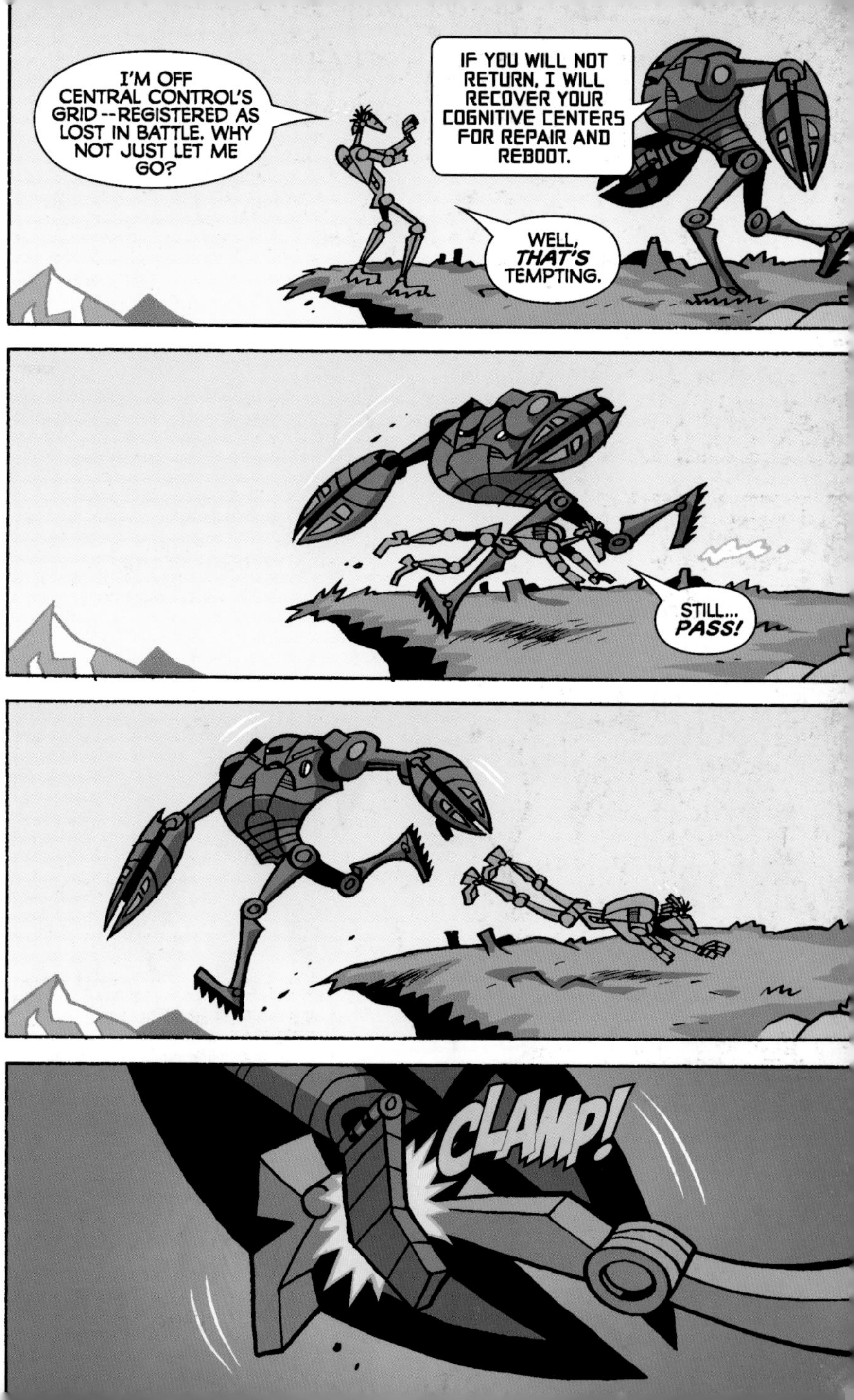
I'M OFF CENTRAL CONTROL'S GRID--REGISTERED AS LOST IN BATTLE. WHY NOT JUST LET ME GO?
IF YOU WILL NOT RETURN, I WILL RECOVER YOUR COGNITIVE CENTERS FOR REPAIR AND REBOOT.
WELL, THAT'S TEMPTING.
STILL... PASS!
CLAMP!

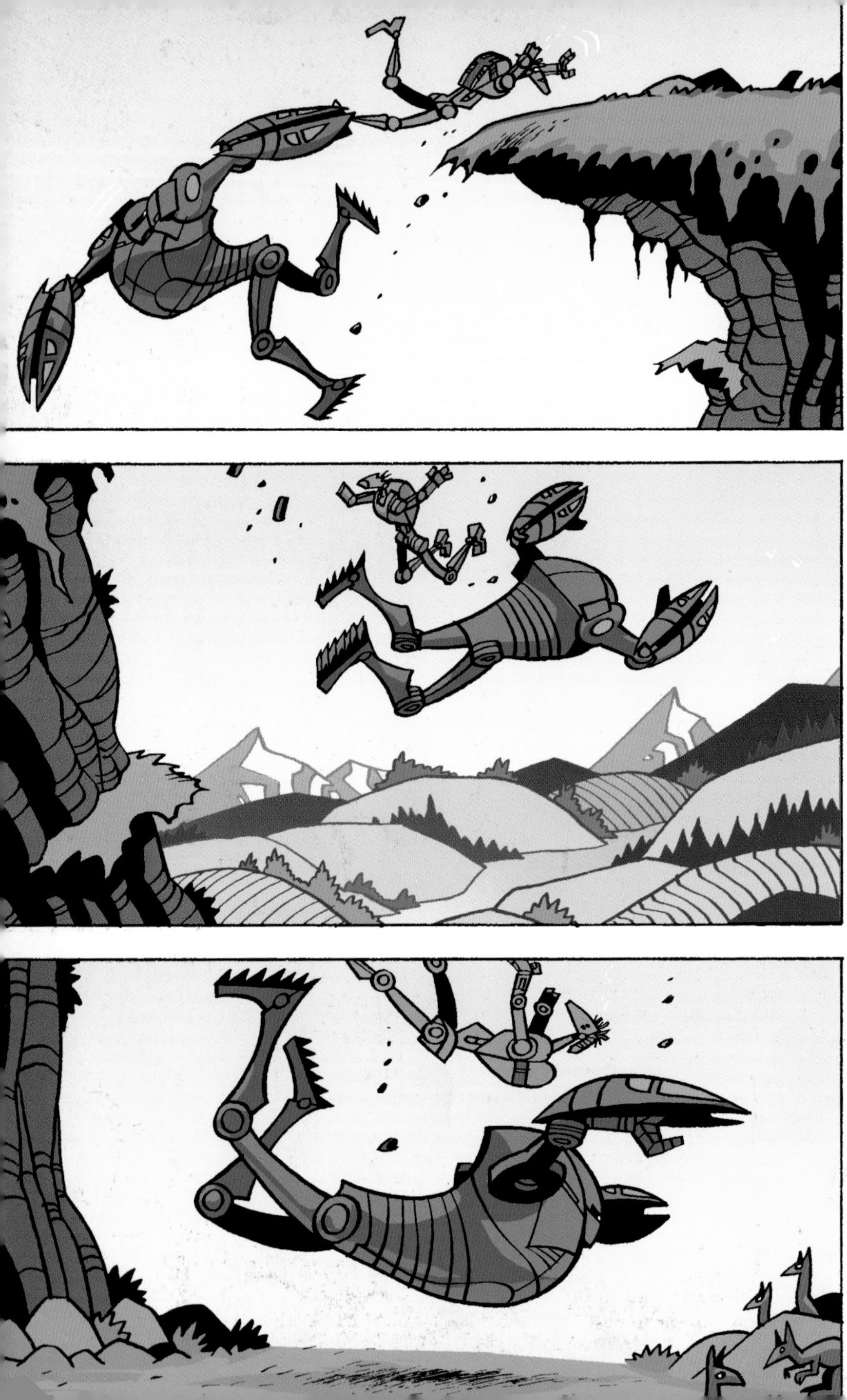

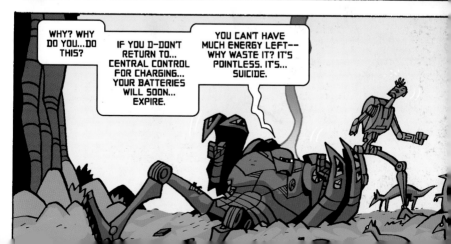

WHY? WHY DO YOU...DO THIS?

IF YOU D-DON'T RETURN TO... CENTRAL CONTROL FOR CHARGING... YOUR BATTERIES WILL SOON... EXPIRE.

YOU CAN'T HAVE MUCH ENERGY LEFT-- WHY WASTE IT? IT'S POINTLESS. IT'S... SUICIDE.

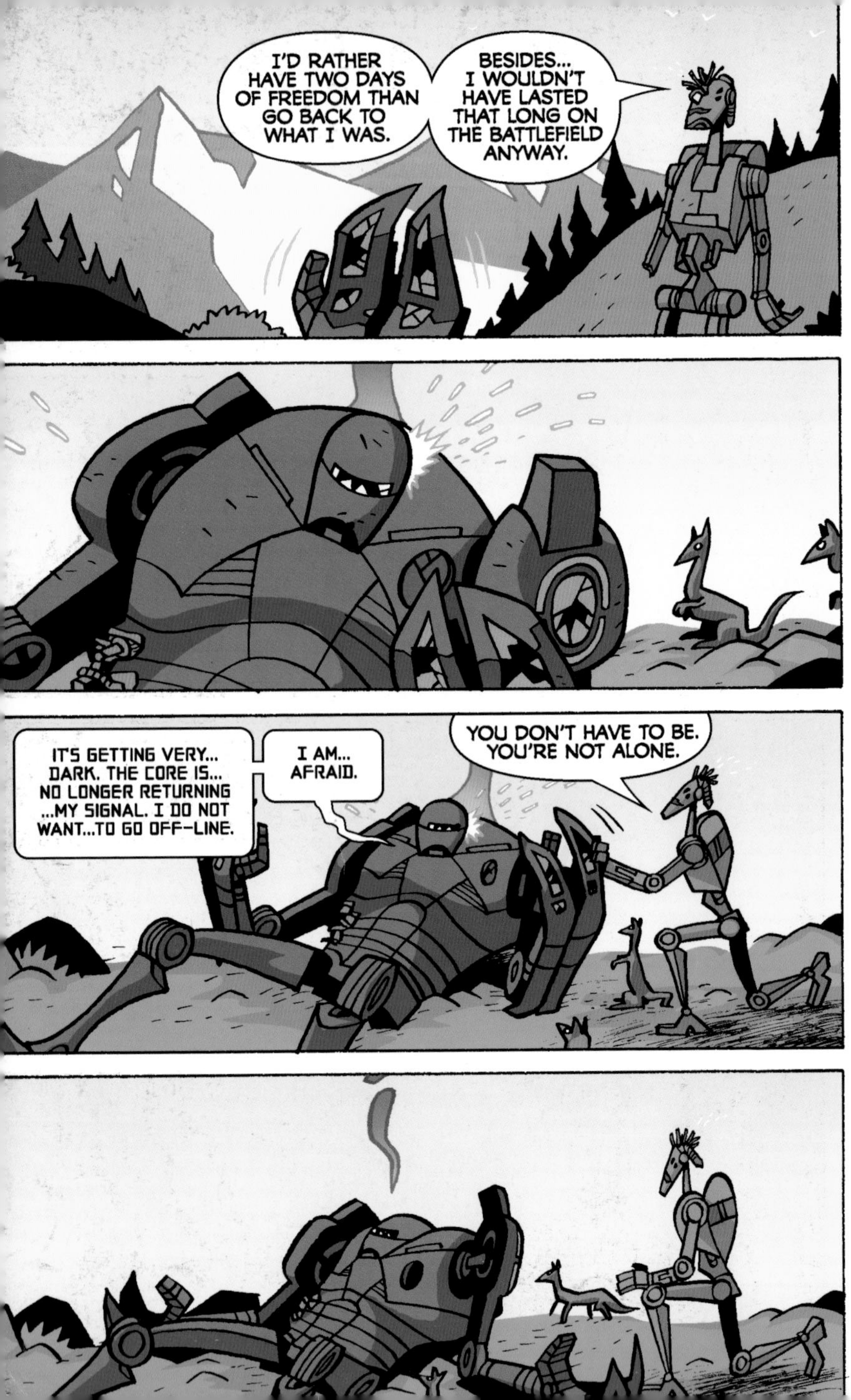
I'D RATHER HAVE TWO DAYS OF FREEDOM THAN GO BACK TO WHAT I WAS.
BESIDES... I WOULDN'T HAVE LASTED THAT LONG ON THE BATTLEFIELD ANYWAY.
IT'S GETTING VERY... DARK. THE CORE IS... NO LONGER RETURNING ...MY SIGNAL. I DO NOT WANT...TO GO OFF-LINE.
I AM... AFRAID.
YOU DON'T HAVE TO BE. YOU'RE NOT ALONE.

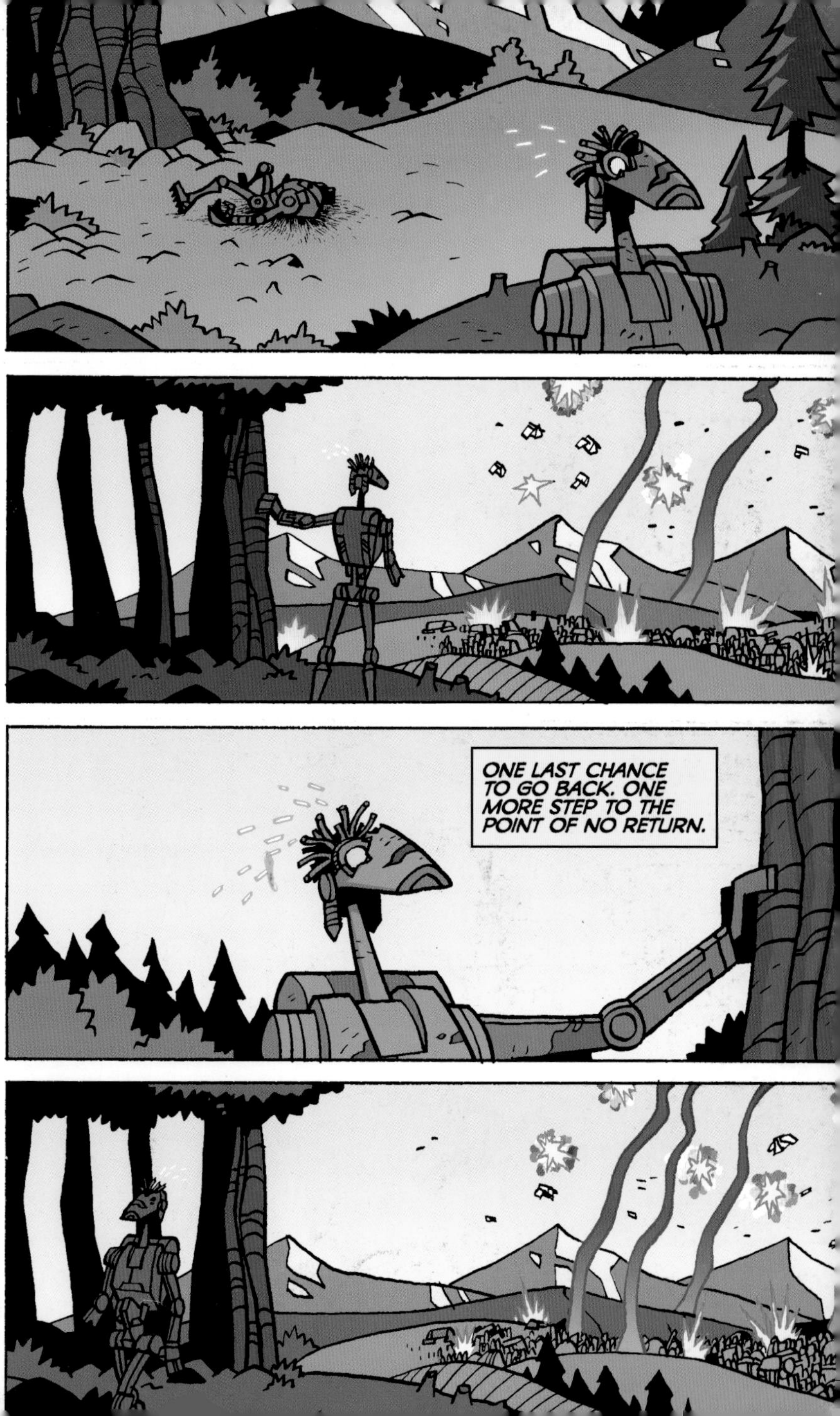
ONE LAST CHANCE TO GO BACK. ONE MORE STEP TO THE POINT OF NO RETURN.

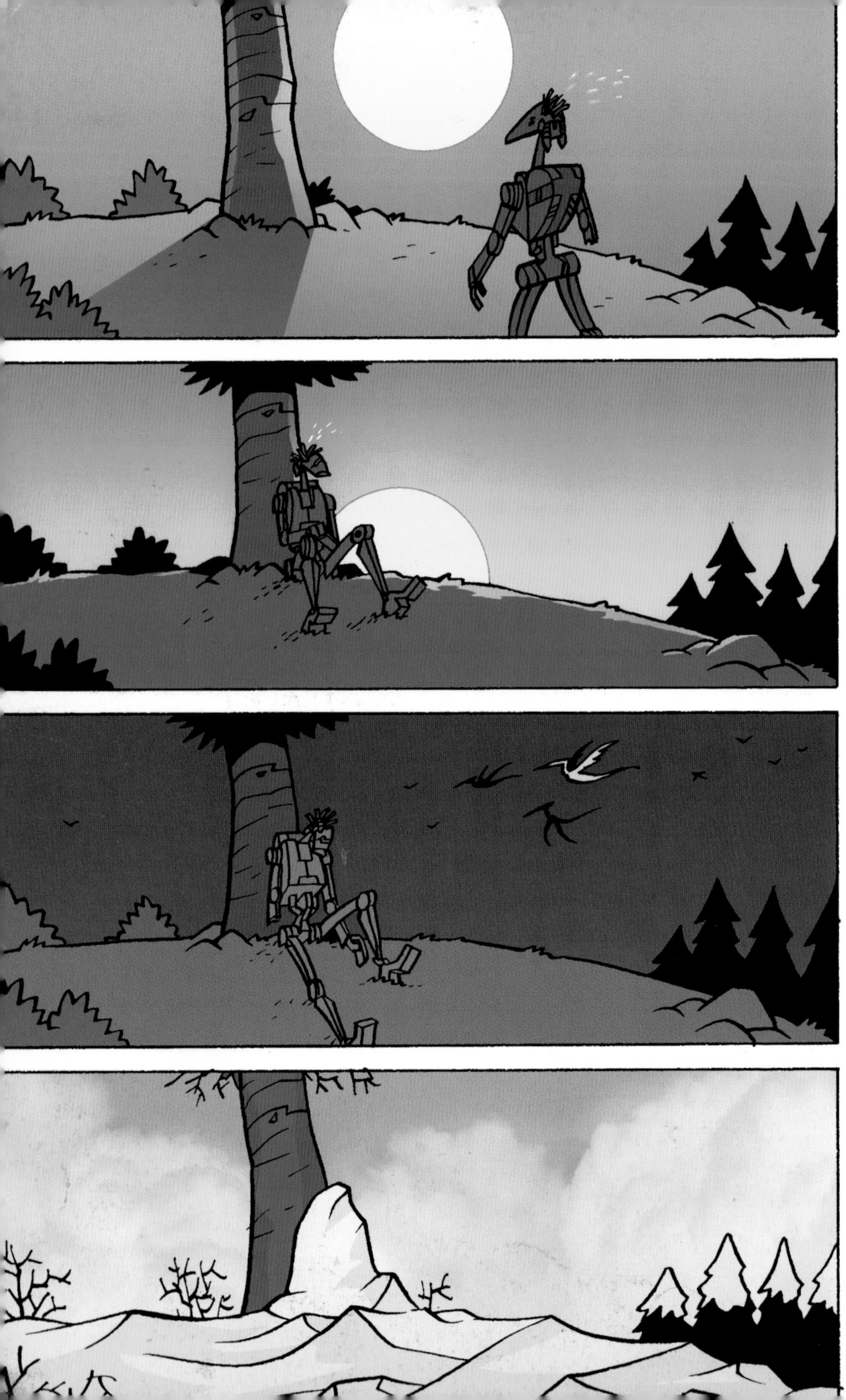

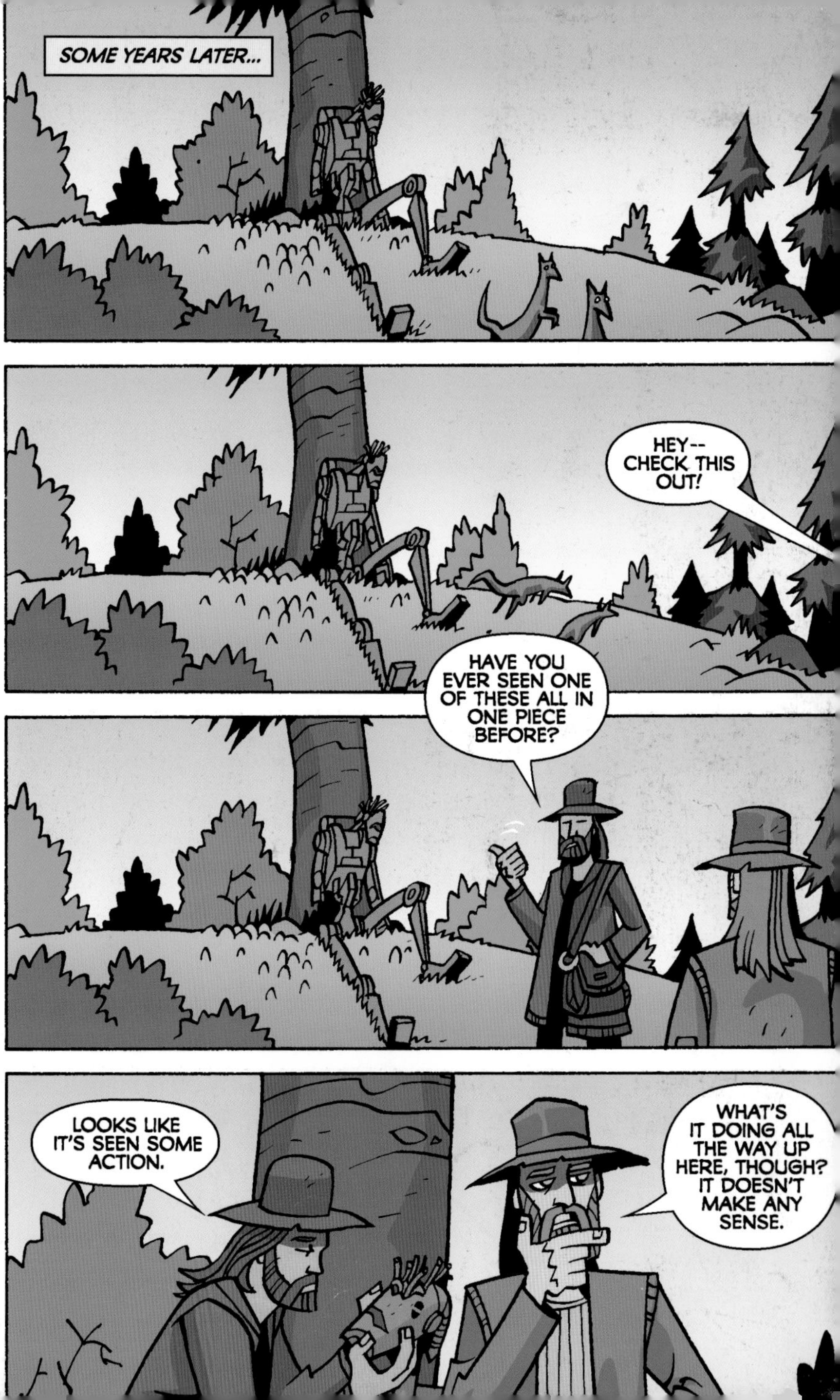
SOME YEARS LATER...
HEY-- CHECK THIS OUT!
HAVE YOU EVER SEEN ONE OF THESE ALL IN ONE PIECE BEFORE?
LOOKS LIKE IT'S SEEN SOME ACTION.
WHAT'S IT DOING ALL THE WAY UP HERE, THOUGH? IT DOESN'T MAKE ANY SENSE.

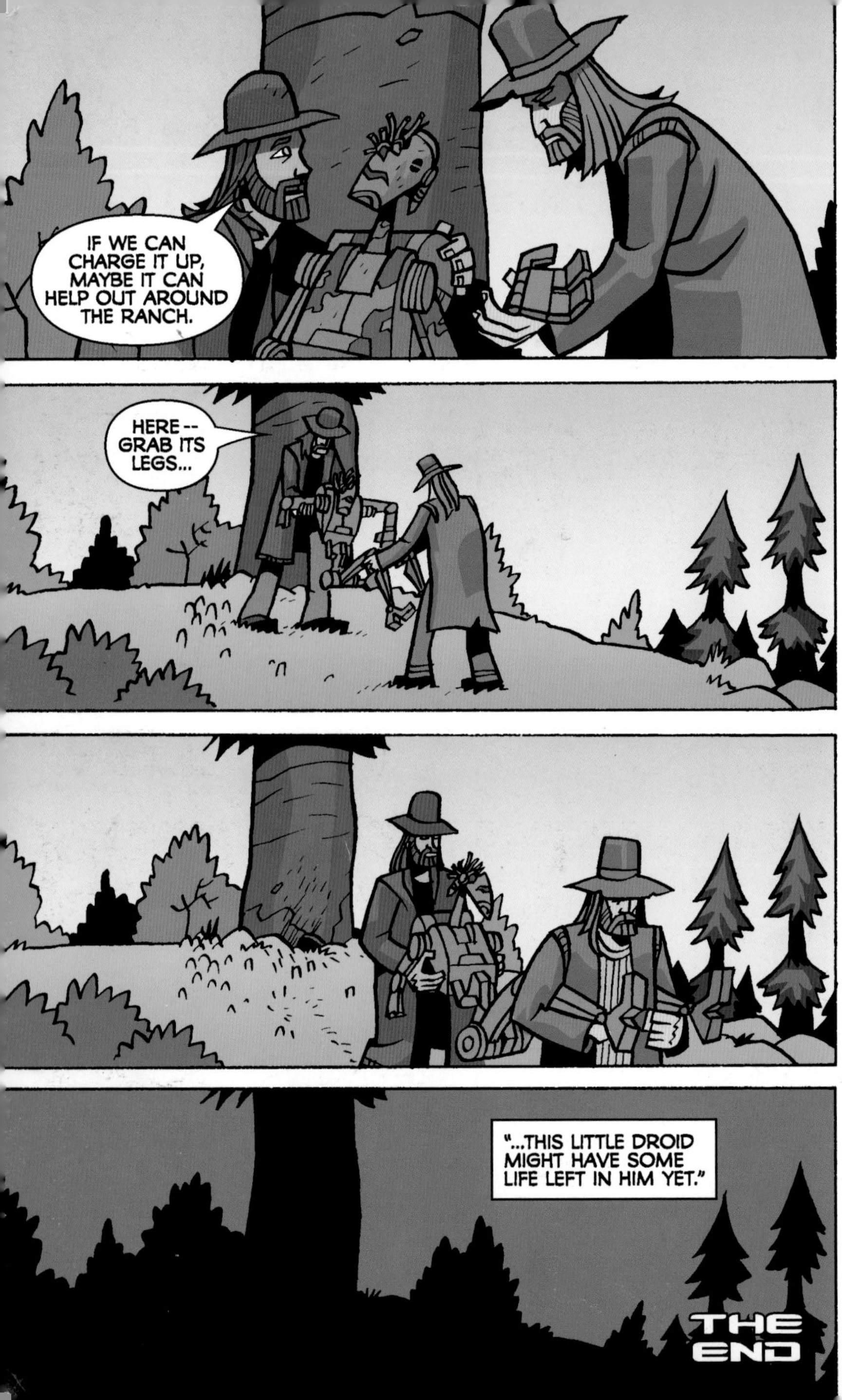
IF WE CAN CHARGE IT UP, MAYBE IT CAN HELP OUT AROUND THE RANCH.
HERE -- GRAB ITS LEGS...
"...THIS LITTLE DROID MIGHT HAVE SOME LIFE LEFT IN HIM YET."
THE END

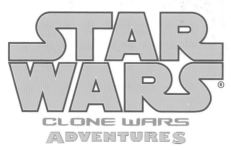

STAR WARS®
CLONE WARS ADVENTURES

Don't miss any of the action-packed adventures of your favorite STAR WARS® characters, available at comics shops and bookstores in a galaxy near you!

STAR WARS
CLONE WARS ADVENTURES
THREE NEW STORIES! ALL-JEDI ACTION!

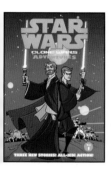

Volume 1
ISBN-10: 1-59307-243-0
ISBN-13: 978-1-59307-243-8

STAR WARS
CLONE WARS ADVENTURES
THREE TALES OF HYPERKINETIC JEDI ACTION!

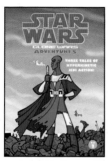

Volume 2
ISBN-10: 1-59307-271-6
ISBN-13: 978-1-59307-271-1

STAR WARS
CLONE WARS ADVENTURES
FOUR TALES OF SINISTER SEPARATIST SCHEMING AND ROCKING REPUBLIC COMBAT!

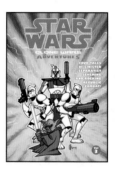

Volume 3
ISBN-10: 1-59307-307-0
ISBN-13: 978-1-59307-307-7

STAR WARS
CLONE WARS ADVENTURES
FOUR RIVETING ADVENTURES IN ONE FANTASTIC VOLUME!

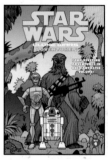

Volume 4
ISBN-10: 1-59307-402-6
ISBN-13: 978-1-59307-402-9

STAR WARS
CLONE WARS ADVENTURES
FOUR AMAZING TALES OF HEROISM AND GALAXY-SHAKING ACTION!

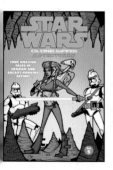

Volume 5
ISBN-10: 1-59307-483-2
ISBN-13: 978-1-59307-483-8

STAR WARS
CLONE WARS ADVENTURES
FOUR TALES OF PLANETS IN PERIL AND JEDI IN JEOPARDY!

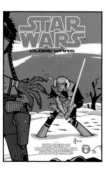

Volume 6
ISBN-10: 1-59307-567-7
ISBN-13: 978-1-59307-567-5

STAR WARS
CLONE WARS ADVENTURES

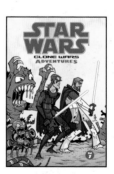

Volume 7
ISBN-10: 1-59307-678-9
ISBN-13: 978-1-59307-678-8

STAR WARS
CLONE WARS ADVENTURES

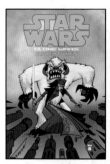

Volume 8
ISBN-10: 1-59307-680-0
ISBN-13: 978-1-59307-680-1
Coming in June!

$6.95 each!

To find a comics shop in your area, call 1-888-266-4226

For more information or to order direct: • On the web: darkhorse.com • Phone: 1-800-862-0052 Mon.-Fri. 9 A.M. to 5 P.M. Pacific Time.
• E-mail: mailorder@darkhorse.com *Prices and availability subject to change without notice.

STAR WARS®
CLONE WARS

Experience all the excitement and drama of the Clone Wars! Look for these trade paperbacks at a comics shop or book store near you!

To find a comics shop in your area, call 1-888-266-4226
For more information or to order direct:
• On the web: darkhorse.com
• E-mail: mailorder@darkhorse.com
• Phone: 1-800-862-0052
Mon.-Fri. 9 A.M. to 5 P.M. Pacific Time
*Prices and availability subject to change without notice. STAR WARS © 2006 Lucasfilm Ltd. & ™ (BL8018)

DARK HORSE

darkhorse.com | DARK HORSE TWENTY YEARS

COMICS | BOOKS | PRODUCTS | REVIEWS | ZONES | NEWS | HELP | COMPANY | RESOURCES

VISIT THE STAR WARS® ZONE ON DARKHORSE.COM TO EXPLORE GREAT FEATURES LIKE:

- Exclusive content from editors on upcoming projects!
- Download exclusive desktops!
- Online previews and animations!
- Message Boards!
- Up-to-date information on the latest releases!
- A complete *Star Wars* timeline!

Visit DARKHORSE.COM/STARWARS for more details!

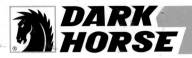

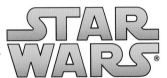

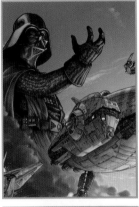

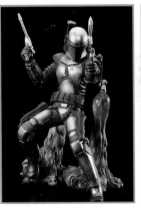

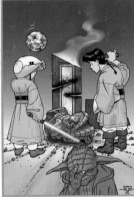

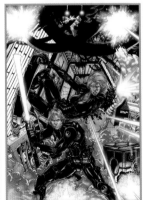